AF574582
SILVER ROADWAYS LTD
SILVER ROADWAYS
LTD.
BER. 4533
39
AEC
KYK 247

BRITISH LORRIES 1945-1983

Cover: A Bedford TM 3800 Tractor unit for hauling 32ton loads (38ton gross combination weight) in service with a Sussex operator. Bedford, Cummins, or Detroit Diesel engines can be specified for these units. *R. Jenner Hobbs*

Below: The latest addition to the Ford Cargo range are vehicles with either Deutz or Perkins V8 engines. The 32½-ton articulated truck shown here has a Deutz 3220 engine.

BRITISH LORRIES 1945-1983

S.W. Stevens-Stratten FRSA

LONDON

IAN ALLAN LTD

First published 1983

ISBN 0 7110 1300 4

Published by Ian Allan Ltd, Shepperton, Surrey; and printed by Ian Allan Printing Ltd at their works at Coombelands in Runnymede, England

Below: A new Leyland Constructor eight-wheeler used for the transport of refuse. Although using the Leyland name and cab, the vehicle was built at the Scammell works.

Contents

Introduction

In updating this completely new edition by six years, one is conscious not only of the changes which have been made in the design of heavy commercial vehicles, but also of the fact that there are now less British makes on the roads. Two factors have caused this; first the great influx of vehicles produced by foreign manufacturers in direct competition with our own motor industry, and partly as an indirect result of this, the dearth of British manufacturers either through financial collapse or as a result of a merger or takeover. In particular many have been swallowed into the British Leyland empire. In 1945, the beginning of this pictorial survey, there were 27 manufacturers; by 1982 this has decreased to 11, although due to joint ownership this figure is actually only nine firms. Of this nine, four are under American ownership and one French, leaving only Dennis, ERF, Leyland and Shelvoke as completely British.

There have been one or two additional firms which produced a few goods vehicles during the period covered by this book — Argyle, Hillmaster, Proctor and Rowe — but their production was so small as to be virtually insignificant and all ceased after a period of only a couple of years or so.

Designs, as can be seen in the photographs that follow, have changed considerably during the 36-year period beginning with the continuation of the prewar models with small improvements. As the industry got into its stride in the civilian market, following experience with military vehicles and other wartime products, and with a steady flow of new materials, entirely new models began to appear. Vehicles became larger , more powerful and more refined, but the technical development also kept apace of the times, as did the safety factors and the provision for the driver's comfort.

Nationalisation of the road haulage industry in 1947 saw the end of many interesting haulage operators and some distinctive liveries. Fortunately at that time many companies in the manufacturing and distributive trades operated their own fleets and thus retained some variety of both makers and liveries.

When the British Railways network was cut back under Dr Beeching, road transport flourished and with the advent of the motorways the commercial vehicle came to reign supreme for the transport of goods from door-to-door, whether in the form of the small humble parcel or the bulk load. The range of operation has further been extended beyond the shores of the British Isles by the roll-on, roll-off ferries between the UK and the Continent and our entry into the European Economic Community both of which have served to give new impetus to Continental work. Even when the railways are involved in the carriage of freight in the form of container traffic, much of this starts and finishes its journey on the rear of a lorry.

It does not seem possible that 26 years ago a lorry weighing more than 3ton unladen was not permitted to exceed 20mph, but the Construction and Use Regulations which govern the design, size and weight of vehicles have gradually been relaxed in accordance with modern requirements, although I feel sure that some operators would like to see them abandoned altogether!

As they have become larger the media seem to refer to all commercial vehicles as 'Juggernauts' — a term which I feel is unjust and inappropriate. The dictionary states that a Juggernaut was a chariot taken in procession, when thousands contended the honour of dragging the vehicle, while many devotees threw themselves under its wheels to be crushed! It can also refer to a relentless inhuman force which destroys blindly anything that comes in its way; hardly fair comment on drivers of heavy goods vehicles who are, generally speaking, among the finest on our roads today.

Modern legislation demands that all commercial vehicles are fitted with tachographs which record the hours worked, the distance covered, the speed, the number of stops and their duration. Drivers are not allowed to drive more than a certain number of hours, unlike the early days when a driver could be behind the wheel for 24 hours or so. Apart from the hours, he was subjected to much discomfort — no windscreen, inclement weather, noise, fumes, a hard seat and poor springs — to name but a few!

The modern cab has comfortable adjustable seats, air conditioning, radio and controls designed to be light and east to reach. Sleeper cabs are also common today and some have facilities for cooking. The vehicles themselves have excellent brakes and suspension, and possibly automatic transmission and power assisted steering.

This modern technology has made some components such as automatic transmissions, turbocharged engines etc, more complex, but steps have been taken to ease the task of maintenance. Tilt cabs which give immediate and improved engine accessibility were introduced in 1962. The greater use of light alloys, fibre glass and plastics has meant that corrosion and rust are virtually eliminated. Engines are more powerful and are thus likely to work under less stress than their predecessors. Standardisation, whilst possibly taking away some of the interest for the enthusiast when applied to visual items like cabs and bonnets etc, can also assist in maintenance and spare parts problems.

It is to be regretted, however, that with ever increasing costs the colourful liveries, hand-applied lettering and lining on vehicles is now becoming a thing of the past and the art of signwriting is becoming a dying trade. The modern vehicle is often in a single colour with the owner or operator's name in a simple Gill Sans (no frills) typeface.

At the time of writing the economic recession has had its effect on the commercial vehicle industry. Many firms are working a three-day week and with a general reduction in manufacturing of all commodities there is less call for road transport; thus operators are purchasing fewer vehicles and making their existing ones last a little longer. Fuel economy is now of major importance and we feel that this is the field for development in the next decade.

This book does not cover the small vans and pick-up trucks which are basically a modified private car chassis, neither does it cover the specialist off-the-road vehicles, which are in a different category. Minibuses and small personnel carriers have again not been included as these really come within the passenger vehicle scene.

I would point out that the illustrations are in no sense to be regarded as showing all the models produced by the various manufacturers in the past 36 years, but merely an interesting selection chosen to depict some of the more important changes of design which have evolved with the emphasis on vehicles seen on the roads in the 1970s and 1980s. In selecting the photographs I have endeavoured to show typical vehicles, not prototypes, one-off bodies, or manufacturers' retouched photographs . All photographs are from the Ian Allan Library or my own collection. Where dimensions have been given, it is hoped that they may be of some use to the many enthusiasts who make models of road transport vehicles.

S. W. Stevens-Stratten, FRSA
Epsom, Surrey

Abbreviations and Glossary

gvw	Gross vehicle weight (rigid vehicles)
gcw	Gross combined weight (usually articulated vehicles meaning maximum weight at which it can operate)
gtw	Gross train weight (trucks and trailers, maximum weight to be towed including towing vehicle)
Forward control	No protruding bonnet — driver sits over or alongside engine
Normal control	Driver sits behind engine which is under bonnet in front
Cab-over	American expression, the same as forward control
Conventional	American expression, the same as normal control
Hood	American name for bonnet
Fender	American name for wing or mudguard
bhp	Brake horse power
mpg	Miles per gallon
4×2	Four-wheeled vehicle, two of which are driven
4×4	four-wheeled vehicle with drive to all four wheels
6×4	Six-wheeled vehicle with drive on four wheels

AEC

The foundations of the Associated Equipment Company date back to 1906 and the Vanguard Bus Company, one of the many independent operators which joined the large London General Omnibus Company; thus AEC commenced to manufacture buses for the streets of London and from 1912 produced the immortal B type bus of World War 1 fame. A lorry chassis was produced in 1916 for use by the Forces, known as the Y type, which was also sold in the civilian market after hostilities were over. This was the beginning of commercial vehicle manufacture for AEC which continued to become one of the largest builders of buses and lorries in the UK.

The company moved from its original works at Walthamstow to Southall in Middlesex in 1927. At this time it had a brief merger with the British Daimler, beginning in 1926 and the name Associated Daimler (ADC) lasted for two years.

During the 1930s AEC was producing vehicles with payloads of 6ton to 13½ton, each model bearing a name such as Mercury, Majestic, Mammoth, Mammoth Major and Mandator, many of these names being carried on the range until lorry production ceased.

During World War 2 production was switched to War Department requirements and AEC produced 9,620 Matador 4×4 medium artillery tractors, 514 Marshall six-wheel 2,500gal refuelling tankers for the RAF, 192 Marshall six-wheel vehicles, many of which had a Coles Crane mounted, 185 similar vehicles for mobile oxygen plants, 629 armoured cars plus diesel engines for the Valentine tank and many other items vital to the services and the country generally.

The return to civilian production in 1948 saw the range consisting of the Matador and Monarch, both four-wheel vehicles for a 12ton gross weight, but with the former capable of hauling a trailer; the Mammoth Major six-wheeler for 19ton gross and the eight-wheeled version with the same name capable of a 22ton gross weight.

1912-1979

AEC took over the old established firm of Maudslay Motor Co Ltd of Alcester (near Coventry) in 1948, also Crossley Motors Ltd of Manchester. Soon after there was a change of name to Associated Commercial Vehicles Ltd, but the initials AEC were kept on the vehicles. In 1949 ACV acquired the body-building firms of Park Royal Vehicles and its subsidiary Charles H. Roe of Leeds, but as both were engaged on bodies for passenger vehicles, it had little effect on commercial vehicle production.

In 1953 an older name was revived — the Mercury — for an 8ton payload with a cruising speed of 40mph. A Park Royal-designed cab was later fitted and appeared on all models about this time.

With large development in the building of motorways and civil engineering generally, AEC entered the earth-moving field in 1957 and produced a large six-wheel, 10cu yd Dumptruck, later building several sizes including an 18cu yd four-axle model. Production of these vehicles under the AEC label ceased around 1967.

Another acquisition was made in 1961 when Transport Equipment (Thornycroft) was absorbed into the ACV empire and production of the normal range of commercial vehicles under that name ceased, although the specialised vehicles such as airport fire-fighting tenders and the Mighty Antars for oilfield and off-the-road work continued.

In August 1962 Associated Commercial Vehicles merged with Leyland Motors and although the AEC range continued it slowly lost its identity, the first outward sign being the adoption of the Leyland Ergomatic cab in 1964 and production was gradually rationalised to avoid undue competition. Finally the name AEC disappeared from commercial vehicles in 1977 (although it continued on buses and coaches for another 18 months or so); the Leyland Marathon being made at Southall until the factory finally closed its gates in 1979.

It is tragic that AEC, founded in 1912 and known throughout the World as 'Builders of London Buses' is no longer in existence, being the victim of a Leyland takeover.

Left: An AEC Mammoth Major eight-wheeler fitted with a six-cylinder, 9.6litre oil engine, capable of dealing with a 15ton payload. This design was outwardly little changed since it was first introduced in 1933. The vehicle was supplied to a well-known transport contractor in the early 1950s.

Top: The Mercury 8ton gcw chassis was introduced in 1953 and less than a year later was carrying the redesigned cab shown here, which was quickly fitted on all AEC models. In 1955 the Mercury was uprated for a 10ton payload and was available with four different wheelbases and a choice of two sizes of engine.

Above: This Mandator tractor and semi-trailer could carry a payload of 32ton and this 1965 example is in the grey and yellow livery of Ferrymasters whose vehicles traverse Europe.

Above: This Marshall six-wheel chassis has an 11cu yd tipper body. It was supplied to a South London contractor during the 1960s. Note the articulation of the rear bogie and the one-piece windscreen.

Left: The Majestic was in effect a lengthened Mandator having a 19ft wheelbase and twin-steering front axles for a 10-11ton payload.

Above right: The London Brick Company had a large fleet of Mammoth Majors for the carriage of loose bricks. Nowadays most of their loads are on pallets.

Right: The Marshall rigid six was available as a 6×2 or 6×4, with a choice of three different wheelbases and six- or 12-speed overdrive gearbox. This 1968 model was fitted with an AEC AV505 diesel engine developing 154bhp. The vehicle has the Leyland-designed Ergomatic cab.

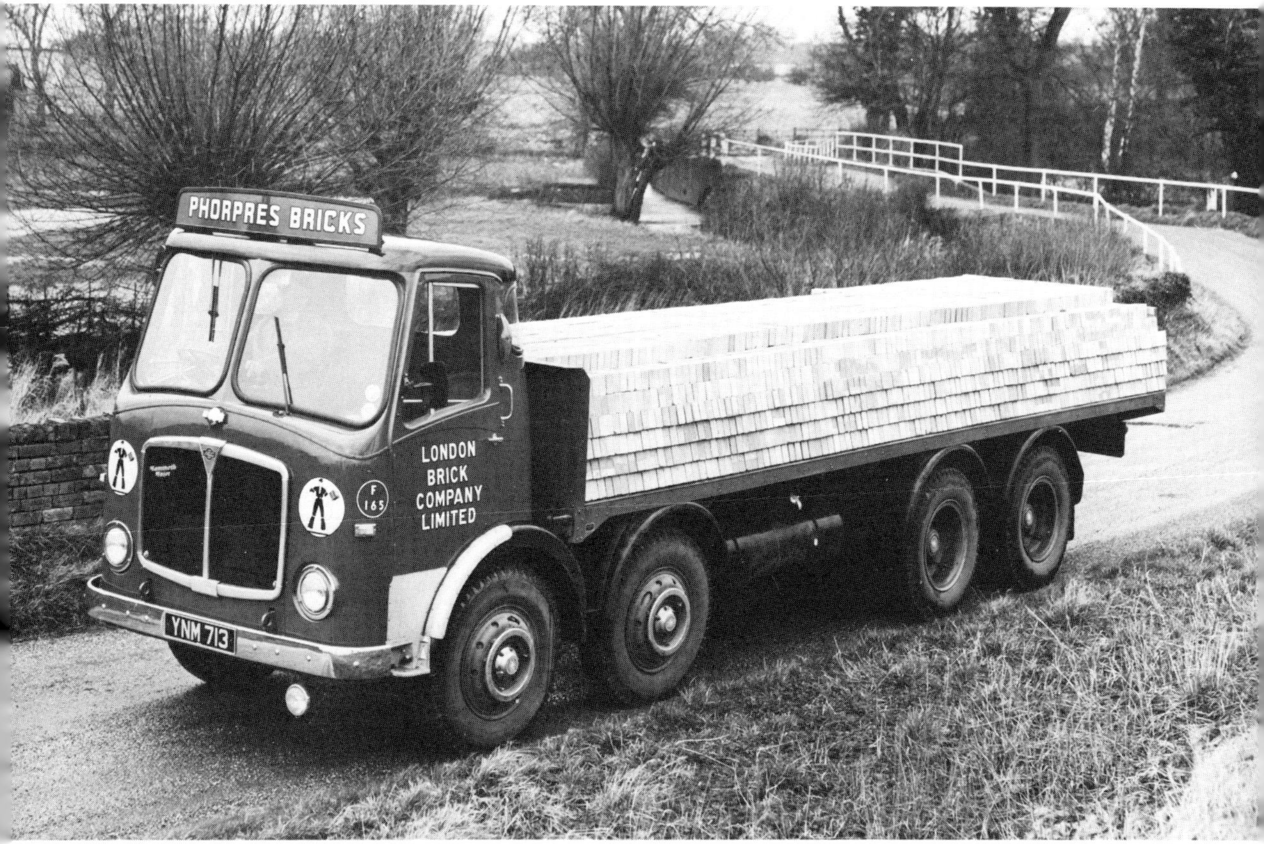
PHORPRES BRICKS
LONDON
BRICK
COMPANY
LIMITED
F
165
YNM 713

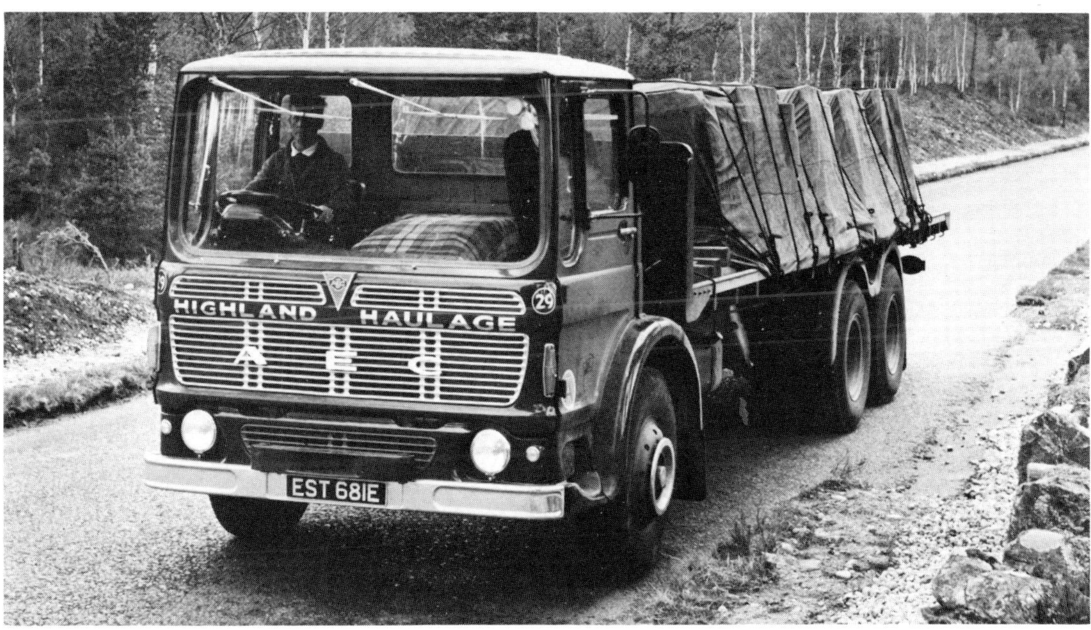

HIGHLAND HAULAGE
29
A E C
EST 681E

Above: A Mandator prime mover for 32ton gcw. This was fitted with a V8 engine giving 272bhp. Six- or 10-speed semi-automatic transmission could be offered as alternatives.

Right: One of the range of dumptrucks which AEC built. This one has a 5cu yd capacity and is working on an opencast site where it could take an average payload of 28ton.

Albion 1901-1972

The Albion Motor Car Co Ltd was formed at Scotstoun, near Glasgow in 1901 and a year later produced its first commercial vehicle which was really a motor car with a body adapted for the carriage of goods. By 1910 it had developed the A10-model truck which had a carrying capacity of 3ton, powered by a 32hp engine, and the model remained in production for 16 years giving the firm much publicity and establishing the reliability and ruggedness of the Scottish product with the slogan 'Sure as the Sunrise'.

During World War 1 the company manufactured thousands of subsidy-type lorries for the War Department, continuing production on an even larger scale when peace returned. In 1931 the word 'Car' was dropped from the company name. The small firm of Halley, which manufactured vehicles in a small plant at Yoker, near Scotstoun, was absorbed in 1935.

Wartime production of Albions consisted of 3ton 4×4 trucks and the 10ton 6×4 bonneted tractor for tank transporters. Production of civilian types recommenced in 1947 with a range of six chassis — the CX7, an eight-wheeler for a 14½ton payload; the CX5 a six-wheeler for 12ton payload; the CX1 and CX3, 7ton and 6½ton four-wheelers, and two lighter models — the FT3 4-5ton and AZ5 for 1½ton loads. Improved versions and other models followed at intervals during the next few years, but in 1951 the company was acquired by Leyland Motors and although production continued the Leyland influence gradually made itself felt. This was noticeable in the cab design and from 1968 the outward appearance of the old Albion features had virtually disappeared.

In 1955 Albion introduced the Claymore a 4/5ton chassis with an underfloor engine — a Leyland O.300 diesel unit . As this was mounted amidships it enabled the cab to be built forward of the front axle, thus giving a good turning circle with the maximum body length for the size of the vehicle — an ideal combination for local delivery and collection work. The Caledonian 16½ton payload rigid-eight was introduced in 1958 and was generally a competitor to the Leyland Octopus.

By 1972 the name Albion had disappeared, to be replaced by Leyland, although the plant at Scotstoun is now producing many of the smaller vehicles in the Leyland range — the Redline in particular.

Below: A 6½ton Albion which although delivered to its operator in 1951 was still the same basic design as prewar vehicles: It was used for the distribution of bottled beers and mineral waters.

Above: A Super Reiver 6×4 chassis fitted with light weight tipping body for the carriage of bulk grain.

Right: Carrying a special body for the transport of pigeons, this Chieftain Super Six was fitted with the Leyland 400 engine. The body was of fibreglass while the whole of the roof was translucent, admitting natural light. The chassis had been extended by 5ft to give an overall length of 34ft.

Below right: A Clydesdale 1,750gal milk tanker, one of a very large number purchased for the bulk collection of milk from farms. The electric motor for the pump was driven by high capacity batteries which were charged by the vehicle's engine during normal running.

Above: The Claymore was popular for suburban collection and delivery work. This is a 4ton model with a 72hp horizontal diesel engine; the body has a capacity of 644cu ft.

Below: This 20ton Reiver bulk grain carrier was delivered in 1968. It had full pneumatic discharging equipment and the dimensions of the body were 7ft 8in wide, 4ft 10in deep and 21ft long which with the boxed headboard gave a capacity of 700cu ft. The vehicle has the Leyland type Ergomatic cab.

Above: A Super Clydesdale tractor and semi-trailer which had a plated gtw of 22ton for UK operation.

Below: At the Scottish Motor Show in 1957 this Caledonian eight-wheeled chassis was fitted with a 3,900gal tank for the transport of transformer oil. Note the Leyland influence in the cab design.

Atkinson 1916-1970

Edward Atkinson, the founder of the firm was an engineer of some repute and from 1907 became an expert in repairing and servicing steam vehicles as well as being an agent for Alley and McLellan, the forerunner of Sentinel. In 1916 he designed and built his own steam wagon — a 6ton, four-wheeler and in the early 1920s was manufacturing about three wagons a week with a staff of nearly 150. However, the economic depression of the late 1920s caused the company to flounder and it was reconstituted as Atkinson Lorries Ltd in 1933 for the production of diesel-powered vehicles using the Gardner engine. Production was small and financial difficulties were ever present. Luckily, wartime contracts for 160 six-wheel and 100 eight-wheel vehicles saved the company and after the cessation of hostilities it was able to relaunch its range of four-, six- and eight-wheeled vehicles, the design of which remained basically unaltered until 1953, when the cabs were redesigned with the familiar bow front.

In 1957 heavier vehicles were marketed with an eye to cross-country and oil-field operations, and the Omega bonneted 6×6 100ton vehicles with Rolls-Royce engines were produced. In 1958 fibre glass cabs which incorporated a wrap-round windscreen were fitted to most of the range.

During the early 1960s Atkinson began manufacturing the Black Knight range of four-, six- and eight-wheeled freight vehicles, the Gold Knight chassis for tippers and concrete mixers (short wheelbase) and the Silver Knight tractor units. During 1968 some Atkinson vehicles were produced with a German Krupp-manufactured cab on a Silver Knight chassis for the European market, but the UK production consisted of the Borderer 4×2 tractor unit, the Searcher rigid-six and the Defender rigid-eight, plus the Omega bonneted 100ton heavy tractor. In 1966 the Viewline cab was introduced, but it was not very popular with operators and was dropped a few years later.

In 1970 Atkinson was finally acquired by Seddon, but production continued and in 1972 the Leader rear-steering tractor unit was launched along with a large 8×4 tipping lorry chassis using the Gardner 150 engine, which was also fitted in some other trucks of larger size. During the early 1970s the Searcher 6×4 chassis proved popular for cement mixers. The emphasis, however, was on tractor units, the Venturer 6×4 and the Borderer 4×2 chassis being offered with a choice of engines, although usually those by Gardner or Cummins were fitted.

Seddon Atkinson was taken over by International Harvester of America in 1974, that firm already having a European interest when it acquired a holding in the Dutch DAF concern.

Vehicles are now marketed as Seddon Atkinson and the 400-series is a range of 12 models — six tractors, a 30½ton and 32ton gcw (with Gardner, Rolls-Royce or Cummins engines); a 30½ton and 32ton gtw four-wheeler capable of towing a trailer; a 24ton gvw rigid-six and a 30ton rigid-eight, (Gardner or Cummins engines for all the last three types). Sleeper cabs can be provided on all chassis. There is also the 200-series of 16ton rigid-fours with choice of three wheelbase lengths all of which have the International engine fitted. Recently the Atkinson 'Big A' motif has been reintroduced on the larger members of the Seddon Atkinson range.

Above: An Atkinson 15ton payload eight-wheeler supplied in 1954 and having the same external appearance as vehicles supplied prior to 1939. Painted dark green with yellow lettering it had a smart and dignified appearance.

Below: A Silver Knight tractor unit operated by a well known Scottish haulier. The 20ton payload unit was fitted with a Rolls-Royce diesel engine.

Top: New in 1960 this Silver Knight eight-wheeler and trailer could carry a 22ton payload at a steady 52mph on motorways. The glass fibre cab is above a Gardner 6LX engine developing 150bhp transmitting its power through a ZF six-speed gearbox.

Above: Model T746X a $7\frac{1}{2}$-8ton tractor of 1960 coupled to a York Freightmaster tandem-axle box van lightweight semi-trailer. It was used for the transport of crated beer.

Above: One of 17 such vehicles built in 1963 especially for gritting and salting the motorways in inclement weather.

Below: An Atkinson tractor on heavy haulage duties. The 43ton load, which was 93ft long was being taken from Glasgow to Treforest.

Austin

1910-1968

The first commercial vehicles made by Austin were 15cwt models based on a car chassis but in 1913 a 3ton truck developing 29hp from its four-cylinder engine was produced. It was a forward-control vehicle and possibly far in advance of its time. Apart from a few odd models in the early 1920s and light delivery vans on car chassis, the Austin Motor Co did not compete in the commercial field until 1938/9 when it commenced manufacture of a range of 30cwt, 50cwt, 2-3ton and up to 5ton vehicles. The heavier models had an appearance not unlike that of their competitors, Bedford, so they became known as the 'Birmingham Bedfords'.

During the last war Austin produced its K2 vehicles in large numbers for use as Army ambulances and also for emergency fire tenders which towed a trailer pump. Austin also produced the K3 4×2 3ton general service lorry, the K6 6×4 chassis used as aircraft refuellers etc and the K5, the 4×4 general duty lorries which soon became nicknamed 'screamers' on account of the noise emitted from the four-wheel drive mechanism and gearbox.

After the war Austin came into its own and a vast number of K2 3ton chassis were produced together with the K4 five-tonner plus the unique three-way forward-control van (type K8) which had a payload of 25cwt with a 2litre petrol engine (an alternative Perkins diesel engine was offered later). Production of this type continued until 1954.

In 1952 Austin and Morris merged to form the British Motor Corporation and some unification of the two ranges began. Identical vehicles could be seen with the badge of either Austin or Morris on their radiators, although as a rough guide Austin appeared on normal-control and Morris on forward-control vehicles. See also the chapter on BMC.

Below: An Austin 2ton van of 1957 operated by British Road Services (Parcels) Ltd. The bodies incorporated alloy panels, the floor was of wood, and the one-piece roof was translucent plastic.

Above: A 4ton forward control chassis with a Bonallack light alloy Luton-type box body. The vehicle was 21ft long and 9ft 8in high.

Below: A modified 25cwt three-way van utilised by Austin for a tour of UK dealers.

Top: A type FJ 18ton gtw prime mover powered by a 120bhp 5.7litre BMC underfloor diesel engine and five-speed direct-drive gearbox to BMC two-speed axle. The semi-trailers were built by Carrimore and delivered in 1965.

Above: A one-ton Austin van with body capacity of 235cu ft. It was available with petrol or diesel engine. The $1\frac{1}{2}$ton version had a capacity of 275cu ft but was virtually the same with 8ft $4\frac{1}{2}$in wheelbase, an overall length of 14ft $7\frac{1}{4}$in and height of 7ft $8\frac{1}{2}$in.

Above: This 3ton parcels van was designed in 1958 by BMC and BRS, the latter using many hundreds of the type. Known as 'Noddy Vans' the chassis was modified with drivers' foot controls moved back 11in and steering altered accordingly to enable driver to enter and leave his seat without climbing over the wheelarch. The body had a 600cu ft capacity and a floor height of only 3ft 3in. The cab was fitted with a sliding door and the driver could walk through to the rear.

Below left: Driver's cab of the type VA 'Noddy Van' showing access to the walk-through cab.

Below right: Introduced in the late 1960s the FF series was for a 5ton payload, but was later uprated. Engine was either a BMC petrol or diesel developing 90 or 105bhp.

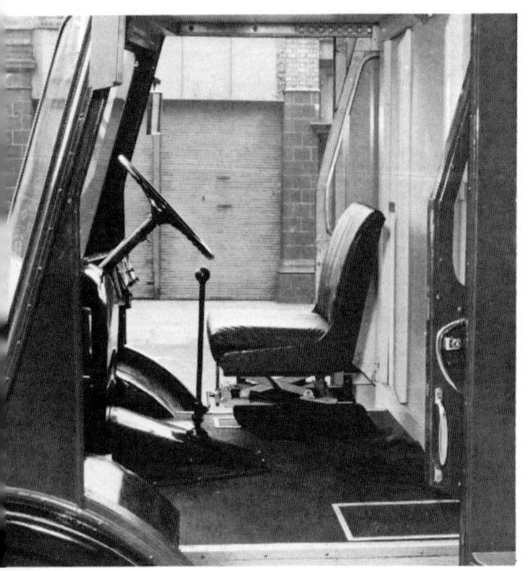

Bedford

1931-To date

The Vauxhall Iron Works produced marine engines and from 1902 became increasingly involved in the new petrol-engined cars. A move to Luton and a change to complete car production proved successful and in the late-1920s the business was acquired by the American giant, General Motors. This company had been struggling to import its Chevrolet trucks into Great Britain, so this acquisition proved to be a turning point; the Chevrolets were redesigned for the British market in 1931 and vehicles were produced at the Vauxhall plant at Luton under the name Bedford. The 2ton lorry with 26hp six-cylinder petrol engine was an immediate success and by 1939 a range of vehicles from 12cwt to 5ton was available.

In 1938 a redesigned radiator grille with rounded front was introduced which became the hallmark for many years, although during the war years a civilian version of the military OY-series, designated the OW-series, appeared with a straight utility bonnet and radiator grille.

Production for the War Department totalled some 250,000 trucks the most numerous being the 15cwt (pneumonia wagon), the 3ton 4×2 GS truck and the forward-control 4×4 QL model.

Manufacture for the civilian market was resumed in 1947 with the same prewar models and in 1950 the first of the Big Bedfords appeared — the 7ton S-type semi-forward control with a new cab and differing wheelbases; there was also a short wheelbase 8ton tractor unit.

In 1960 a radical new design appeared, the now famous TK range with the engine mounted longitudinally immediately behind the drivers cab, thus giving full forward control. New 8cwt vans using many components from the Vauxhall Viva cars were made in 1964. Two years later the KM range for up to 24ton gvw were produced taking Bedford into the heavy market, and this was increased for 32ton gcw when tractor units were introduced in 1972.

In 1976 the production of the TJ bonneted range which started in 1962 ceased. This was superseded by the JM range and in 1978 the TK 4×2 and 6×2 range was extended from 5½ton to 16ton gvw. Changes again took place in 1980 when the TK range was joined by the tilt-cab TL range, which brings Bedford in the forefront of modern design. The old Bedford motto — 'You See Them Everywhere' — still holds good today.

Below: A 5ton Bedford van of the 1950s. This vehicle operated by a well-known toy firm was fitted with a Pallet-Jekta telescopic floor for palletised loading.

Above: Introduced in 1952 the CA 10/12cwt van was an immediate success and produced for over two decades. It was powered by a 1594cc petrol engine as used in the Vauxhall Wyvern car.

Below: In the early 50s when the Bedford range was redesigned some models were then known as the 'Big Bedford'. This S-type tractor unit used by a London grocers was fitted with a Adrolic anti-jack knife stabiliser.

Above: A 1957 Big Bedford 6cu yd tipper

Left: In 1959 the normal-control range was redesigned. Here is a 6ton tipper traversing some rough terrain.

Above: The TK range from 2ton to 12ton tractor units. This is a 1965 model of a 2ton chassis with Hawson box van body for collection and delivery work.

Below: A 2,600gal tanker on a 13ft 2in wheelbase KM tipper chassis. The tank has five compartments and the roller-shutter locker on the nearside houses delivery hoses etc.

Above left: The CF series of vans was introduced for the 1970s and bears a close resemblance to the American General Motors vehicle. It is available for 18, 22, 25 and 35cwt loads. This is a one-ton model powered by a 1.8litre petrol engine used by the Scottish Gas Board.

Left: A 1982 model of the CF chassis. This CF350D small truck is fitted with an aluminium box body and is on contract hire to W. H. Smith from Toller Hire.

Below: Designed for a maximum weight of 38ton the TM3800 is the 'Big Bedford' of the 1980s. Fitted with a sleeper cab, the TM can be fitted with Bedford or Cummins engines.

BMC

BMC — British Motor Corporation — was founded in 1952 following the merger of Austin and Morris (whose entries should be consulted) and these two concerns began to integrate their designs, although for the first four years both continued to market their own models. The BMC letters appeared on some models from 1956, notably the 7ton forward-control trucks (which also had the Austin or Morris badge), then when the British Motor Corporation merged with Leyland in 1968 the BMC name was used for two years but was dropped from 1970 when the larger vehicles became Leyland and the small vans and pick-up trucks reverted to Austin Morris. More recently this latter sector of the British Leyland empire became known as Freight Rover.

Below: The EA type van was a 30cwt nominal payload vehicle with walk-through cab and underfloor engine (70bhp petrol or 66bhp diesel) and was available in two body lengths.

Right: The Mastiff 16ton rigid four-wheeler powered by a Perkins V8 engine. The vehicle has a tilt cab and was one of the largest to carry the BMC badge. It is now marketed as a Leyland.

BROOK DYEING CO. LTD.
BROOK DYEING CO. LTD.
HEAD OFFICE: BOTTOMS MILLS
HOLMFIRTH
Nr. HUDDERSFIELD
36
MASTIFF
B M C
YWY 659G

Bristol 1952-1964

The Bristol Tramways & Carriage Company was founded in 1887 and ran its first motorbus in the Bristol area in 1906. It manufactured its own vehicles from 1908, many being also sold to outside operators. Later the company was acquired by the Thomas Tilling Group of bus operators, which was nationalised in 1947, passing into the control of the British Transport Commission (BTC). As a result of this Bristol only produced passenger vehicles for the nationalised bus companies.

In 1952 Bristol produced its first goods vehicle chassis for the Road Haulage Executive, later to be renamed British Road Services, the goods haulage side of the BTC.

The first goods vehicles were rigid eight-wheelers with a maximum carrying capacity of 22ton (the heaviest permitted at that time). Powered by the Leyland O.600 diesel engine of 125bhp they used gearboxes, transmission and other parts of Bristol manufacture. Later the cab was redesigned and a total of 517 rigid units was produced.

An articulated prime mover was introduced as model HA6L with a Leyland O.600 engine and this was also used by British Road Services.

Production of all goods vehicles ceased in 1964 (buses continuing) and Bristol was later denationalised when British Leyland took a substantial shareholding. Later, a new connection with the nationalised passenger sector was made, when Bristol became part of Bus Manufacturers (Holdings) Ltd, a joint undertaking of British Leyland and the National Bus Company. Its bus products are still available on the open market, however. It is worth noting that this Bristol company had no connection with motor cars of the same name, as that was a subsidiary of Bristol Aircraft.

Below: One of the earlier Bristol rigid-eights fitted with the Leyland O.600 9.8litre engine.

Above: A Bristol tractor unit and semi-trailer for BRS, with an overall length of 34ft 6½in.

Below: A tractor unit positioning a Roadrailer at a railhead. The road wheels are about to be raised and the rail wheels lowered for coupling to the trailer at the rear to form the train.

Commer

Commercial Cars Ltd was founded in 1907 and had a chequered career. It was moderately successful in its earlier days, then financial troubles overtook the firm and it was taken over by Humber Cars in 1926, which was itself acquired by the Rootes Group in 1928. The name was abbreviated to Commer and the 1930s proved successful. Just prior to the war it introduced the Superpoise range of popular and well-designed vehicles.

The Commer contribution to the war effort produced over 20,000 vehicles for the three services, including the tractor units for the 60ft long 'Queen Mary' semi-trailers used by the RAF for the carriage of aircraft fuselages and wings.

Resuming production of the normal-control Superpoise after the war it added a Commer-Hands 6-8ton tractor and semi-trailer unit, and the normal control 25cwt van, which shortly afterwards became available as a forward-control model. In 1948 a redesigned range was put on the market with underfloor engines for 5ton and 7ton payloads, both being full forward control. A new two-stroke diesel engine was marketed in 1953 having two horizontally-opposed pistons in each of the three cylinders. This engine was fitted to certain of the range, but alternative Perkins diesel engines of conventional design were also offered. The Superpoise range was extended in 1955 with 2-5ton

vehicles with a six-cylinder diesel engine while the 15cwt and 25cwt vans had a four-cylinder engine.

A delivery van of exceptional merit was introduced in 1961 for $1\frac{1}{2}$-3ton payloads; this was the Walk-thru van with semi-forward control and it remained in production long after the name was dropped.

A range of forward-control medium-weight vehicles appeared in 1963 later to be superseded by the V range. In 1966 Commer entered the heavier market with a 16ton gcw chassis and cab, having produced the Maxiload tractor unit for 12ton lorries in 1962.

In 1964, the American giant Chrysler got a foot into the Rootes empire, gaining complete control in 1973. Chrysler, which already owned Dodge in the USA and which firm had made trucks in the UK since 1933 (see separate chapter) somewhat naturally decided to market all the Commer range as Dodge, thus the old established name of Commer disappeared from 1976 except for a few municipal vehicles which also appeared under the Karrier name. These changes had already partly been put into practice when the Commando models were marketed as Karrier in 1974.

In 1978 the French Peugot-Citroen Group purchased the Chrysler European interest, but to date there have been few outward changes.

Left: A 5ton Superpoise tipper with 4cu yd body capacity. This model was fitted with a Perkins P6 diesel engine. There is little difference to cab and bonnet design from the prewar model.

Top right: A Commer $1\frac{1}{4}$ton forward-control van of 1956 with a distinct Karrier-style front end.

Centre right: A 12ton tractor unit fitted with TS3 engine coupled to a 2,000gal tanker delivered in 1955.

Bottom right: The new Superpoise normal control 3/4ton chassis introduced in 1956.

Right: One of the last Commer designs — a 8ton platform lorry of 1962. The wheelbase was 15ft 7in.

Above: The well known Walk 'thru van. This is the $1\frac{1}{2}$ton model (the 2ton has twin rear wheels, but is otherwise the same. It has a Rootes diesel engine developing 56bhp. Overall length 17ft 2in, width 6ft $9\frac{1}{4}$in, height 5ft $9\frac{5}{8}$in and wheelbase 10ft 3in. The price complete in 1961 was £952.

MABEY
MABEY
TELEPHONE VICTORIA 8025 (6 LINES)
COMMER
555 ELF

Dennis

John Dennis commenced building cycles in 1885 and bought his younger brother Raymond into the rapidly expanding business. It was a simple step from cycles to the early motorcycles (called Speed Kings) and thus on to motorcars. Dennis Brothers of Guildford produced its first commercial vehicle in 1904 and had two 14hp two-cylinder models and 20, 24 and 28hp four-cylinder vehicles also available two years later. Fire engine production actually started as early as 1908 and a year earlier it had produced a worm-drive 5ton lorry.

The War Department $3\frac{1}{2}$ton subsidy lorry of 1913 was produced in large numbers and following these the $2\frac{1}{2}$ton chassis was used for municipal vehicles such as refuse collectors, gully emptiers, cesspool emptiers etc.

By 1918, Dennis had acquired the well known Coventry engine manufacturer, White and Poppe,

but did not enter the heavy market in the 1920s; even in the 1930s it was concentrating on the 2ton-6ton range with the exception of the six-wheeled 12-tonner introduced in 1931. In 1933 Dennis produced its popular Ace models which became known as 'Flying Pigs' because of the protruding snout-like bonnet ahead of the front axle. A heavier vehicle, called the Max, appeared in 1937 having a payload of 6-8ton and full forward control.

Wartime production was large numbers of trailer fire pumps and various vehicles for the services.

Production resumed in 1946 with the Max and the Pax 5ton, both of which were prewar designed, and a new 12ton six-wheeled chassis called the Jubilant which had a five-speed gearbox and a 7.6litre engine later enlarged to 8litre. This later engine also powered the Centaur forward-control 6-7ton rigid lorry introduced in 1948 and the 12ton Horla tractor unit.

In 1954 Dennis produced a new design of 3ton payload van with an underfloor engine, called the Stork, but it does not appear to have been very popular. The Max was replaced by the Hefty in 1957 and also the Centaur by the Condor for 7ton payloads. The heavy market from 1964 was supplied with the Maxim — a four-wheel rigid 16ton and a six-wheel 22ton gvw vehicle of similar type but again this does not appear to have been very successful. However throughout this period the production of fire appliances and municipal refuse collectors using the Paxit compressing system was considerable.

At a time when Dennis was experiencing the closure of its bus building activities and with less sales of commercial vehicles it was acquired by the Hestair Group which injected capital into the organisation.

During the mid- to late-1970s the emphasis was on the establishment of a completely new passenger range, but production of refuse collectors, fire appliances and other municipal/specialist vehicles continued, with a very limited production of general haulage vehicles to special order. However in 1979 the Delta 16ton freight chassis for tipper and general haulage applications was revitalised with a new metal cab and went into full-scale production, albeit in smaller quantities than those of other manufacturers. Like most current Dennis products it is available with a wide range of engine/gearbox options.

Left: A normal control Pax 5ton vehicle supplied in 1945, continuing the prewar design.

Above right: Few examples of the Centaur tractor were built. This one dates from 1954 and was fitted with a $5\frac{1}{2}$litre engine.

Right: A 1958 forward control Pax II fitted with a petrol engine. It had a loading height of only 3ft 3in.

Below: Ten years on from the previous illustration — a Pax V chassis and cab for a 15ton gvw.

Above: A Pax II model of 1961 vintage for carrying a non-vintage beverage!

Left: This 3ton underfloor-engined Stork had a light alloy body with a cubic capacity of 950ft. It was delivered in 1954.

Right: Not unlike the Stork is this Heron removals van of 1960.

Below: This Pax fitted with a Perkins P6 oil engine, supplied in 1957, was notable for its modern cab design.

Dodge

1922-To date

The American company Dodge Brothers was assembling its imported parts in Britain in 1922 and in 1933 commenced manufacture of British chassis, but with American engines and gearboxes, at its works at Kew with its associated company, Chrysler. In the mid-1930s it concentrated on production of a semi-forward-control design of lorries and achieved some success with a 4-5ton short-wheelbase tipper. There was also a 30cwt van and a 2ton lorry.

After the war production recommenced at Kew with a range from 2ton to 6ton with a cab similar to that fitted to the Leyland Comet and in 1957 a 7ton chassis was offered with a Perkins R6 engine. An entirely new range made its appearance in 1956/7, of normal-control outline, and two years later a range of forward-control vehicles extended the range to 22ton gvw. These vehicles used proprietary parts such as Perkins engines and Motor Panels cabs as used on some Leyland and Albion models.

When Chrysler finally gained control of the Commer concern in 1973 there was much changing of badges and in 1976 the Dodge badge appeared on Commer-designed vehicles from the 1¼ton Spacevan to the 7-12ton Commando.

The Kew plant closed in 1967 and all production was switched to the Commer/Karrier plant at Dunstable. Further changes still took place and in 1980 the K series with tilt cabs were withdrawn.

Below: A Dodge 2/3ton van supplied in 1948 to the same design as prewar models.

Top: With a cab similar to some Ford models, this Dodge tractor unit had a Perkins engine and was delivered to its operator in 1955.

Above: A 3ton van of 1953. Fitted with a 114bhp petrol engine it has a light alloy body which was finished in yellow and blue. The bonnet and radiator have a similarity with the Leyland Comet.

Right: A forward control 5ton van of 1958. The wheelbase was 13ft 7in and the body had a capacity of 1,200cu ft. It had a glass fibre reinforced plastic roof.

pierre
Imans figures
ures"
Paris
pierre
Imans figures and fashion decor ltd.
10/16, RATHBONE STREET,
OXFORD STREET,
LONDON, W.1.
PHONE: MUS: 5300.
VXB103

Top: The Dodge Walk-Thru van was based on the original Commer design. The model was available in two wheelbases and a choice of three engines and from $1\frac{1}{4}$ to 3ton payload. This model has a Perkins diesel engine and a wheelbase of 10ft 3in.

Above: A 1967 13ton tilt cab tipper with a Perkins 120bhp diesel engine and a wheelbase of 10ft 8in. This is one of the Dodge 500 series of vehicles.

Above: A 100 series Commando lightweight box van with the Hi-Line tilt cab. Models in this range cater for $4\frac{1}{2}$-12ton payloads with choice of Perkins diesel or Chrysler V8 petrol engines.

Below: The 300 series 32ton tractor. Fitted with a Chrysler 11.9litre turbocharged diesel engine and a nine-speed gearbox.

ERF

1932-To date

Edwin R. Foden broke away from the family Foden concern and started to make his own diesel-powered lorries in 1933 using some proprietary units such as Jennings cabs and Gardner engines. The first vehicle was a forward-control four-wheeler for a 6ton payload (type C14) and the model proved so successful that it remained in production until 1946. All ERF vehicles since that time have been forward control and have had conventional radiator grilles and the prewar range catered for 6ton to 15ton payloads on rigid four-, six- or eight-wheeled chassis.

The range continued after the war but with a redesigned radiator grille which was larger and almost flush with the slightly curved cab front which had lower windscreens. Then followed a more streamlined cab with wrap-round windscreen which was introduced in 1949.

In 1952 a completely new design of oval radiator grille was incorporated on all models and this lasted until about 1961 when the LV cab type was introduced. The company produced its first 32ton gcw tractor unit in 1962.

The production of fire appliances was commenced in 1967 and this lasted for 10 years until it was taken over by Jennings, which had always had close links with ERF, as Cheshire Fire Engineering Ltd.

In 1970 the A range was rationalised and in 1974 the B range with steel-framed plastic cabs appeared for the highly successful four-, six- and eight-wheeled rigids and for the four- and six-wheeled tractor units for load of up to 32ton gtw which appeared in 1975. With the increasing use of British lorries on the continent, ERF developed the SP cab in 1973 on vehicles up to 42ton gcw with the Motor Panels sleeper cab as an optional extra.

A lighter version of the B range known as the M range was introduced in 1978 which had the same cab but was a four-wheel 16ton gtw with the option of a Gardner or Dorman engine; this was followed by a six-wheel 26ton rigid.

Below: The classic prewar design of ERF is still very much apparent on this 15ton payload twin-steering lorry delivered in 1953.

Top: The cab design favoured in 1954 is shown on this 15ton eight-wheeled platform lorry. The oval radiator grill is distinctive to ERF at that time. The 18ft wheelbase accommodates a 24ft long body.

Above: An ERF tractor with a Dyson low-loading semi-trailer for heavy haulage.

Above: A type LAC 340 tractor powered by a Cummins oil engine delivered in 1974 for a well-known haulier of liquids. This was the first vehicle to be painted in the operator's new livery of red and green with yellow lettering.

Below: The new B series appeared in 1975. This rigid eight-wheeled tipper is powered by a Gardner 6LXB diesel engine through a David Brown six-speed gearbox and double reduction rear axle. The body is 23ft 6in long and the sides are 4ft 6in high.

Below: A Gardner-powered ERF tractor is the motive unit for this special tanker for the transport of corrosive liquids. The tanks are of nickel steel equipped with a heating blanket covering the entire tank barrel to keep the contents fluid in low-temperature conditions.

Bottom: A 1981 tractor unit fitted with a Gardner 6LXCT turbocharged engine developing 230bhp at 1,900rpm.

Foden

Edwin Foden designed his first steam tractor in 1882 using an efficient design of compound engine and it came into regular production from about 1887. Within 10 years load-carrying steam lorries were on the market and in 1902 production of the famous 5ton lorry commenced which ran until 1923. The superiority of the petrol (and later oil) engine, plus the heavy legislation placed on steam vehicles sounded their death knoll and so in 1931 the company turned its attentions to diesel-powered lorries using the Gardner engine, but later using several different makes of oil engine.

In the eight years up to the outbreak of World War 2 a large number of commercial vehicles were produced ranging from 4ton to 15ton payload and all featuring the same distinctive but conventional design of radiator grille. During the war the company was engaged on supplying 6×4 army

lorries and parts for Centaur and Crusader tanks as well as munitions of various types.

Civilian production commenced as soon as possible after the cessation of hostilities using the prewar types but the cab design was soon modernised with a curved front with the radiator grille blending into the new outline.

In 1964 the Steel Company of Wales placed an order for a large-capacity tip lorry, as a result of which the first of many giant dump trucks were manufactured. The particular model looks small by comparison with those manufactured in later years, but at the time was regarded as huge. In the same year the revolutionary Foden two-stroke diesel engine was produced and production continued until 1977. Further modernisation and development took place in 1956 when power-assisted steering was introduced and two years later Foden unveiled its first vehicles fitted with a reinforced plastic cab, which in 1960 was modified to tilt forward and give complete and unobstructed access to the engine and mechanical components. In 1968 a few half cabs with forward angled windscreens mounted low on the chassis were made for special orders for cranes and the carriage of long girders etc.

A new factory was opened in 1974 for increased production, although later the company ran into financial difficulties, but a large NATO order effected a recovery. New Fleetmaster and Haulmaster models with steel tilt cabs (of Motor Panels manufacture) were introduced in 1977. The Fleetmaster was normally fitted with a Cummins or Rolls-Royce 290bhp engine and the Haulmaster which had a slightly different radiator grille and a split windscreen, was fitted with Cummins, Gardner or Rolls-Royce 180-265bhp engine. These models were also available in 1979 with a glass-fibre and aluminium cab.

In 1980 following a year of financial difficulties the receivers were called in and after negotiations the American company Paccar International (builders of Kenworth and Pacific trucks in the USA) acquired control. The new company is now called Sandbach Engineering Co although the familiar Foden name still appears on all the vehicles.

Left: Delivered c1953 this twin-steer 15ton lorry has the standard prewar Foden cab.

Above: The postwar redesigned cab and radiator grille shown on a FG6/15model eight-wheeled platform lorry.

Below: Keeping a similar style of radiator embellishment this 1958 short-wheelbase eight-wheeler has the rounded type cab.

Top: From cement in bulk to cement in sacks! This FG 6/24 model was powered by a Gardner oil engine and had a five-speed overdrive gearbox. The tyres are 40 by 8.

Above: An unusual Foden van fitted with a four-cylinder two-stroke diesel engine.

Above right: Foden made several vehicles with half-cabs. This dump-truck is on demonstration work in a quarry typical of the conditions for which it was designed.

Right: This Superhaulmaster six-wheeled tipper has a Cummins engine and the Foden S90 all-steel cab. A model of the 1980s.

Below: The Foden S10 sleeper-cab is fitted to this tractor unit delivered in 1979 for long distance haulage. It is powered by a Rolls-Royce 265L diesel engine driving through a Fuller gearbox. The trailer length is 38ft 8in.

Ford

1908-To date

Ford began to export its American cars to England in 1904 followed four years later by the model T lorry, but from 1911 assembly of these began at the company's premises at Trafford Park, Manchester. The model T continued until 1927 when the Ford model A was introduced. A move to Dagenham in Essex took place in 1931 and from then onwards the vehicles were of English design (more or less) and manufacture.

The Ford contribution to the war effort was immense, making Bren-gun carriers and other half-tracked vehicles, the general service 15cwt trucks and 4×4 forward-control three-tonners for the army and the other services. It also produced the six-wheel winch lorries for the balloon barrage, mobile canteens and fire tenders.

The name Fordson was adopted for commercial vehicles from about 1929 and another change of name occurred in late-1939 when the word Thames was introduced in 1957 this became Thames Trader, a name which continued for the next eight years.

The Thames 15cwt forward-control van made its appearance in the mid-1950s and this was the forerunner of the highly successful Transit van which was produced in 1965 and developed from German Ford Taunus vehicles. The original production was in Belgium with assembly at Langley near Slough. The vans were revamped in 1978 and are still in production. The bonneted Thames Trader K series was also introduced in the early 1960s with a range from 2ton to 8ton, some models being available with several different wheelbases. The K-series remained in production until 1972.

The D-series of forward-control vehicles made its appearance in 1965 catering for loads from 4ton to 10ton including a short-wheelbase tractor for use with semi-trailers. The range was redesigned in 1978 and continued in production until 1981 when the new Cargo range was announced.

Ford entered the real heavy market in 1974/5 when it introduced the H range, soon to be called the Transcontinental. These vehicles were originally built in Amsterdam and fitted with a three-man Berliet-built tilt cab.

Below: A Ford Thames van of 2ton payload which could have either a petrol or diesel engine fitted. A 3ton van had similar dimensions but was fitted with larger tyres and servo-assisted brakes.

Above: A 5ton Thames Trader tractor unit of 9ft wheelbase powered by a six-cylinder diesel engine. This semi-forward control cab was used on many models in the Thames Trader range for several years.

Right: The Ford Thames 15cwt van popular with the small retailer in the late 1950s and early 1960s was the forerunner of the Transit van.

Below right: Who said glamour and commercial vehicles don't mix! A Transit van shows its graceful lines! The Transit series is based on six different payload categories, the larger versions having twin rear wheels.

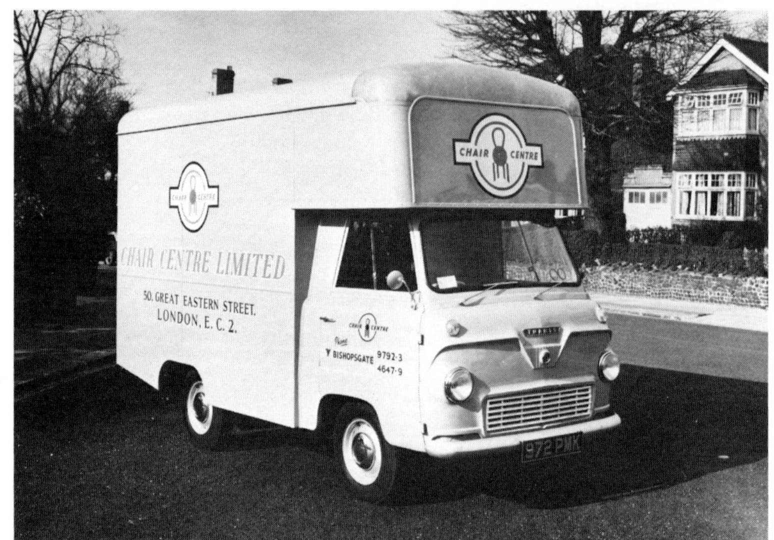

Left: A Ford D-series box van of 1972 which weighs under 3ton unladen and thus does not need a driver with a heavy goods vehicle licence.

Below: A 16ton D-series fitted with a Ford 6litre turbocharged diesel engine. The wheelbase is 17ft 2in. Supplied in 1972 for the delivery of both barrel and bottle beers.

Above right: The A-series provides $3\frac{1}{2}$-$5\frac{1}{2}$ton gvw vehicles which thus fit into the Ford range between the lighter Transits and the heavier D series. This 3ton van is powered by the Ford 2.4litre diesel engine.

Right: The Transcontinental articulated unit powered by a Cummins turbocharged engine with a Fuller nine-speed gearbox. The Transcontinental range is available in 4×2 and 6×4 variants with a choice of wheelbases.

Below: The latest Ford is the Cargo with a range from 6ton to $28\frac{1}{2}$ton gross with a choice of engines and transmissions. The deflector plate on the cab roof is to improve air-flow and is claimed to make a saving on fuel consumption. Such plates are now fitted to a great number of vehicles of all makes.

Guy 1918-1979

In 1914 Sydney Slater Guy left the Sunbeam Motor Co, where he was works manager, and started his own company, almost next door, to produce his own design of commercial vehicles. The new factory was engaged in wartime production almost immediately, but in 1920 vehicle manufacture commenced in earnest with the 25cwt J-type lorries, and later the four-wheel and six-wheel models for 7-12ton payloads. In the early 1930s the Wolf range for 25cwt to 3ton was produced and the 3/4ton Vixen and the 6ton Otter models made their appearance.

The Government ordered large numbers of the angular fronted Quad-ant 4×4 tractors for war use and also allowed Guy to produce a few vehicles for the civilian market to those operators who could claim an urgent need and who had priority.

Full civilian production recommenced after 1947 to prewar designs, but in 1952 a new all-steel cab was fitted to the 6ton Otter model and the following year this vehicle was available as a short wheelbase tractor for use with semi-trailers. A year later the Big Otter was produced for 8ton loads together with the Invincible range of four-, six- and eight-wheeled rigid vehicles for 12ton, 20ton and 24ton gcw respectively.

In 1956 the Warrior range was introduced; these were forward control types for 6ton to 15ton payloads as either rigid or articulated units. From 1958 they shared the same design of cab as the Invincible.

Guy Motors was taken over by Jaguar Cars in 1961, which in turn was taken over by Leyland Motors in 1968. In the interim the Big J series of six and eight-wheeled rigids and tractive units appeared, being a development of some previous models.

Alas, production finally ceased in 1979 and the famous Red Indian figure with the slogan 'Feathers in our Cap' no longer adorns the radiators of products from Fallings Park, Wolverhampton and such radiator caps are now a treasured memento of the past.

Below: This Guy Vixen 4ton platform lorry could carry 80 milk churns. It was supplied to its owners in 1951 and was practically identical to the prewar design.

Above: This 1957 7ton Otter had the new style cab which was virtually the same as that fitted to some Thornycroft models.

Below: An 8ton Warrior van fitted with a Meadows diesel engine and delivered in 1956.

Top: A Warrior articulated unit, fitted with the AEC 7.7litre diesel engine.

Above: A different design of Warrior cab on this tractor unit which hauls a York Freightmaster semi-trailer.

Above: A Big J tractor unit operating at 32ton gtw coupled to a tri-axle semi-trailer milk tanker.

Below: Another Big J tractor unit fitted with a Cummins engine and operating at 30ton gtw. The wide loading side door of the semi-trailer permits pallet loading as shown.

International 1965-1969

In 1965 the Doncaster factory of International Harvester which produced farm machinery commenced vehicle production on Loadstar trucks of a normal-control design. This was based on the American International Paystar, but was modified to comply with UK Construction and Use regulations although fitted with many parts imported from the USA. A few 4×2 rigids were built, together with some articulated tractor units, and a forward-control model was also planned. However the vehicle project did not make sufficient profit and faced severe competition from the European imports; thus all production ceased in 1968.

Below: An International K8 lorry of 6ton capacity in 1943. This vehicle was probably delivered to the UK as ckd (completely knocked down) and assembled here by the International organisation.

Right: Front view showing the American influence of the International model manufactured in the UK in 1965.

Jensen

In the late-1930s the law stated that all vehicles weighing over 3ton unladen must be restricted to a maximum speed of 20mph. Therefore in 1938/9 Jensen Motors of West Bromwich, in collaboration with The Reynolds Tube Company, introduced some lightweight vehicles. These made use of light alloys and aluminium, Ford petrol engines and some parts from the then current Ford 3ton models to produce a lorry which was below 3ton unladen yet could carry a 6ton load at over 20mph.

In 1946 a fresh approach was made. The integral construction of the main frame and the superstructure as one unit in special light alloys allowed the vehicle to have a platform length of 23ft, which could accommodate a 1,632cu ft pantechnicon body on the 16ft 2in wheelbase in an overall length of 27ft 6in — the maximum permitted. Perkins P6 six-cylinder 70bhp oil engines were fitted behind the decorative radiator grille. It also had the advantage that the entire engine complete with radiator, clutch and gearbox could be withdrawn in 30min and a new unit fitted within a two-hour period.

The raising of speed limits and other legislation made the lightweight vehicles unnecessary, and this, plus the high cost of repairs if a vehicle was involved in an accident, proved to be their downfall.

In 1951 Jensen introduced a four-wheel articulated tractor and trailer called the Jen-Tug. This used the Austin A40 private car engine but the vehicles were not popular and few were built.

Production of Jensen Commercial Vehicles ceased in 1956/7 although the company continued to produce some high-class motorcars.

Below: A typical Jensen 6ton payload lorry with light alloy bodywork. The length of the dropside body was 23ft.

Right: This large removal van was fitted with a Perkins P6 diesel engine and was delivered in 1947. The number plate was obviously for photographic purposes!

READS THE REMOVER
PETERBOROUGH
Reads
OF PETERBOROUGH LTD
PHONE 3427/8
READS

Karrier 1908-1980

Karrier has had a chequered career since it began life in 1908 when Clayton & Company (Engineers) of Huddersfield introduced its first lorry under that name. Karrier Motors as a separate entity, being founded in 1920 to continue the motor business, produced a wide range of types including in 1930 the Karrier Cob three-wheel tractor (a mechanical horse) and the Road-Railer bus for the London Midland & Scottish Railway in 1932. However financial difficulties in 1934 caused the company to be taken over by the Rootes Group a year later. Production of commercial vehicles was transferred to Luton and Dunstable alongside the Commer range. A popular prewar model was the Bantam which was designed for payloads up to 2ton and had a low loading height.

During the war a large number of 3ton 4×4 lorries (the K6 type), the KT4 4×4 gun tractor and some rigid six-wheel 3 tonners were built.

The peacetime vehicles were again produced after the war, the Bantam 30cwt and 2ton models having a new cab, while the CK3 model in the 3-4ton range was introduced, but in 1950 these were superseded by the Gamecock with underfloor engine and an all-steel cab identical to that fitted to some Commer vehicles.

In 1963 the Bantam was again updated. The whole of the Karrier range was popular for municipal duties and for suburban collection and delivery services.

The control of Karrier (likewise Commer) passed to Chrysler UK Ltd in 1970 and the firm is now owned by Renault/Peugeot which took over the Chrysler European operations, and it is now partly merged with Dodge.

Below: A 1946 Karrier CK3 model 3/4ton dropside lorry with 14ft 6in by 6ft 8in body on 11ft wheelbase chassis. This is the same as the prewar design and continued for another three years.

Above: An actual exhibit at the Commercial Motor Show in 1952 was this Bantam 2ton mineral water lorry. The cab has been modernised from the earlier models by incorporating rear corner lights and swivelling quarter lights in the all steel cab.

Left: Another example of a Bantam two-tonner, this time with bodywork for a mobile shop, a role for which it was particularly suited.

Top: A Bantam used as a tractive unit and fitted with the Commer diesel engine. It was used for delivery to a retail grocery chain.

Above: One of the later production models of the Bantam, supplied to British Railways for parcels delivery.

Land Rover 1949-To date

The Rover Company produced its first car in 1904 but had never entered the commercial vehicle field. During World War 2 it manufactured many vehicles for the War Department. Afterwards, in 1949, the British Army sought a vehicle similar to the American Jeep, which had proved so successful in numerous wartime campaigns and served in many countries with the British and Allied Forces.

In 1949, therefore the first Land Rover four-wheel-drive vehicle, with a 7ft 4in wheelbase (11ft 11in long), made its appearance. It was powered by a 1,600cc petrol engine and had a payload of 15cwt. in 1952 a longer wheelbase (9ft 1in) version was introduced and a 2litre engine could be offered as an alternative. In 1957 a 2.1litre Rover diesel engine was also made available, and shortly afterwards the 2litre units were increased in size to $2\frac{1}{4}$litre. Land Rovers have been supplied for various bodies, including trucks, hard-tops, caravans, estate vehicles, fire appliances etc. A forward control version is also available.

In 1970 the Range-Rover was introduced again with four-wheel drive (permanently engaged) and powered by a 130hp V8 petrol engine. This is extensively used by police forces in the UK for accident and traffic control work, where its high speed proves an advantage.

The Rover Company became part of the British Leyland empire in 1967.

Below: A normal Land Rover fitted with a metal body — the canvas tilt body was standard — and available with either a petrol or diesel engine.

Above: The long-wheelbase version of the Land Rover shown here with a station wagon body. It is fitted with the Rover V8 petrol engine.

Below: The forward-control model Land Rover which gave increased load capacity and could still traverse rough terrain.

Left: The forward-control chassis fitted with security van bodywork. Note the comparatively short wheelbase for this type of vehicle.

Below: The Range Rover station wagon is used by many police forces especially for motorway patrols and for accidents etc. They can carry a large amount of useful equipment.

Leyland

The vast British Leyland Truck and Bus Division, which has swallowed up so many manufacturers, began making steam wagons in 1896, the first petrol-engined vehicle appearing in 1904 for a 30cwt payload. Then followed the Y-type 3ton and the X-type $3\frac{1}{2}$ton in 1907. The firm established itself in 1912 with the normal-control 3ton subsidy-type vehicle, of which 5,932 were built up to November 1918 for the Royal Flying Corps, the vehicle became known as the RAF type and was sold to many civilian operators.

Leyland has been responsible for many developments in the commercial field over the years, backed by a team of brilliant engineers such as Sir Harry Spurrier, and it thus gained a great reputation for good design and reliability. In the 1930s Leyland was producing freight vehicles with a range extending from the Cub 3ton normal-control model to the eight-wheeled forward-control Octopus for 15ton payloads. Other models were named Bison, Buffalo, Bull, Beaver, Hippo, Lynx and Steer.

During the war years Leyland contributed to the national effort by producing five different types of tank including the Cromwell and Comet as well as supplying 1,000 Hippos and other vehicles and munitions for the fighting services.

One of the first of the new postwar range was the Comet 75 in 1947 — a semi-forward-control 6ton model distinguished by the new frontal styling. Four years later the Comet 90 model for $7\frac{1}{2}$ton loads was made and remained in production until 1960. Super Comet forward-control models appeared in 1954, with cab design similar to that of the Albion Chieftain.

In 1951 Leyland acquired Albion Motors, followed by Scammell in 1955 and AEC (which had already acquired Maudslay, Crossley and Thornycroft) in 1962. Leyland acquired a major shareholding in Bristol Commercial Vehicles in 1965, Rover/Alvis joined the empire in 1966, followed by Aveling-Barford a year later and in 1968 Leyland merged with British Motor Holdings

Below: A Leyland Octopus of 1950 vintage with a special body for the carriage of flour in bulk. The payload of 8ton of flour could be discharged in 45min by compressed air.

which already had Austin, Morris, Guy and Daimler under its wing. Thus many famous makers have disappeared under the Leyland name.

A completely new design of cab was introduced in 1968 known as Ergomatic and this became standard on the heavier models in the range, including those produced under the Albion and AEC names.

In 1970 the goods vehicle range was again extended with the introduction of the Bear six-wheeler and two years later the new Buffalo range of models up to 32ton. The Marathon range of tractive units and 4×2 rigids for loads up to 32ton gcw or 44ton gtw were introduced in 1973 and three years later there was a new Octopus rigid eight-wheeler.

The lighter vehicles known since 1968 as the Redline range were redesigned in 1972 with the Mastiff six-wheeler joining the existing Mastiff (16, 24 and 28ton), the Boxer (10-16ton) and the Terrier $6\frac{1}{2}$-$9\frac{1}{2}$ton). These vehicles were all fitted with the G cab design. The range also incorporated the GF range of lighter vehicles from BMC of $3\frac{1}{2}$-$6\frac{1}{2}$ton. All these models were produced at the Bathgate Works, West Lothian.

One of the latest 1980 designs from Leyland is the Roadtrain (model T45) with five models of forward-control tractive units incorporating a new cab design (type C40) which can also be supplied as a sleeper cab, and the new Leyland Flexitorque engine with Rolls-Royce or Cummins as an alternative.

At the same time there is a normal control Landtrain of which eight models are available from 19ton to 65ton. The models are mainly for the export market and supersede the Super Hippo and Super Beaver.

In 1981 a lighter version of the Roadtrain, called the Cruiser, entered production with a range of three tractive units fitted with a slim version of the new C40 cab and designed for operation up to 34ton gcw. Later that year a lightweight range, also fitted with the C40 cab, called the Freighter was introduced to replace the Clydesdale, and from late-1982 the Boxer.

Below: The semi-forward-control Comet model introduced soon after the war. This one was fitted with a special Holmes light alloy platform body.

FOR COMFORT
HEATING
DIMPLEX
dimplex
FOR COMFORT HEATING
553 DO

Panasonic
Panasonic
LEYLAND
JLW 519V

Above left: The Super Comet forward control was introduced in 1954. This van has illuminated panels made from acrylic sheet.

Left: At the lighter end of the Leyland range is the Terrier with a choice of engines.

Above: With the same G-type cab design as the Terrier, this Boxer is a 1980 model with a turbocharged engine. The vehicle covers over 1,000 miles a week and the wind deflector on the cab roof is intended to make some considerable fuel economy returns, especially on long motorway runs.

Right: A 1980 Bison 24ton six wheeled tipper. The alloy body for sand and rock haulage carries a payload of 16$\frac{1}{2}$ton and a capacity of 12cu m.

Above: Introduced in 1980 this new Leyland Constructor (part of the T45 Roadtrain range) which will supersede the Routeman and Octopus models. This 30ton gross eight-wheeler carries a 20ton payload in the Metalair bulk cement tank fitted with a Holmes blower. The engine develops 209bhp and is matched to the Eaton six-speed gearbox.

Below: P&O Road Services Ltd took delivery of 11 Marathon tractor units in April 1978. Fitted with Cummins diesel engines they haul semi-trailers carrying chemicals.

Top: One of the 1980 Leyland models is the Landtrain, developed chiefly for the export market. Several variations are available.

Above: An extremely long semi-trailer is hauled by this 1980 Leyland Roadtrain tractive unit. The vehicle has the C40 cab, a Leyland TL12 turbocharged engine developing 281bhp and a Spicer 10-speed gearbox.

Right: This Roadtrain hauls a semi-trailer which holds 40cu yd — payload capacity of 20½ton — of bulk grain.

Below: The 1981 introduction was the Cruiser fitted with a 'slim' version of the C40 cab for operation up to 34ton gcw. Three tractive units are available.

Above: The EA type van was introduced in BMC days for payloads of $3\frac{1}{2}$-$4\frac{1}{2}$ton.

Below: The Sherpa van has been universally popular since introduced in 1976. The model illustrated has left hand drive and is operated by a Netherlands butcher. It has a payload of one ton and can be fitted with either petrol, lpg or diesel engine of 1,798cc capacity. The Sherpa received a facelift in 1982

Maudslay 1903-1954

The name Maudslay is well-known among engineering circles of yesteryear for the family became established in marine and steam engines as far back as 1835. It is associated with the beginnings of the Standard cars, and commercial vehicles bearing the Maudslay name were first produced in 1907, being chain-driven for $1\frac{1}{2}$ton and 3ton capacity.

However the company was hit by the depression of the early 1930s and production dropped to a mere 50 vehicles a year. New designs were to have been shown at the cancelled Commercial Motor Show of 1939, but after the war these models were put into production. The range consisted of the Mogul, a 6 ton four-wheeler; the Militant, a 7cu yd tipper; the Mustang, a 10ton rigid twin steer six-wheeler; the Maharajah, a 13ton rigid six-wheeler; the Maharanee, a 13ton tractor unit and the Meritor (originally named the Mikado), a 15ton rigid eight-wheeler.

In 1948 Maudslay was absorbed into the Associated Commercial Vehicle group and for a few years afterwards produced vehicles to its new owner's specification and although a few kept the Maudslay name, most had the AEC badge. Production finally ceased in 1954.

Below: A Maudslay Mogul Mk II of 1948 which follows the style of the other models in the range at that time.

Top: A Mustang twin-steer six-wheeler with platform body. Note the black radiator shell.

Above: A Maudslay Marathon coach chassis was used as the basis of the Harrington-bodied horsebox supplied to British Railways in 1949. It was the prototype for a well-known Dinky Toy model.

Morris Commercial 1924-1954

The name of William Morris, later Lord Nuffield, and the Bullnose Morris are legendary and although the first light vans were produced on private car chassis from 1913, it was not until 1924 that the first real commercial vehicles bearing the name Morris came into being. The first model was a 1ton normal-control type with a 13.95hp four-cylinder petrol engine on a 10ft 2in wheelbase chassis which remained in production until 1932; by a strange coincidence it was designated as the model T — the same as the Ford. Other types quickly followed and in the mid-1930s the models ranged from 10cwt to 5ton. Both normal- and forward-control types were available, some of which had a 'classic' appearance with a slightly pointed radiator grille.

From 1948 the range coped with heavier payloads still, whilst retaining its good looks. Several alternative engines were offered including the 100hp six-cylinder and a new diesel manufactured in association with Saurer.

The popular J-type forward-control van was first introduced in 1949 for 10cwt payloads and two years later the restyled 2/3ton and 5ton models were called Equiload.

In 1952 Morris merged with Austin to form the British Motor Corporation and standardisation began to take place although several Morris designs could be seen with the Austin badge. In 1953 the LD type 1ton and 1½ton vans were manufactured to a design that was finalised before the merger negotiations. See also the chapter on BMC.

Below: This Morris Commercial LC4 series 1½ton drop-side truck is similar to the models made just prior to 1939. It was an improved version of the LC3 series.

Above: A Morris articulated unit delivered in 1957. The whole unit weighed 10ton and could carry 2,400gal of ice-cream.

Below: The FJ-series chassis and cab with Bonallack light alloy Luton body. The body has a capacity of 1,240cu ft closed by an alloy roller shutter at the rear.

Above: Appearing in the mid-1960s Morris J4 10/12cwt vans were used by many traders. This one had an overall length of 13ft 3in, a width of 5ft $9\frac{1}{2}$in and a height of 6ft $3\frac{7}{8}$ with 7ft 2in wheelbase.

Right: A strengthened 7ton chassis was the basis of this tipper/dumper delivered in 1959. It had a four-wheel drive conversion by Martin Harper of Guildford.

Below right: The FG range was fitted with a cab which made reversing easy and made for safer exit on the 'traffic' side of the vehicle. This is a $1\frac{1}{2}$ton truck which shows the angle of the doors. Other models were produced to 5ton payload.

Scammell

1919-To date

The name Scammell is automatically associated with articulated lorries, mechanical horses and heavy haulage. Scammell and Nephew started business as wheelwrights and coachbuilders before producing its first articulated lorry in 1919 utilising lessons and experience gained in World War 1. Scammell Lorries Ltd was founded in 1922 and began producing articulated tanker vehicles. In 1931 rigid six-wheelers were also added to the range and in the late 1920s the first of a long line of heavy and rugged tractor units appeared which were especially designed for the haulage of very heavy and out-of-gauge loads.

Scammell became famous in 1933 for the design and production of its mechanical horse, later the Scarab, which was updated in design in 1945 and continued in production until the 1960s, by which time it had acquired a glass-fibre cab.

During the war Scammell produced the Pioneer tractor which was used for tank transporters, recovery vehicles and artillery tractors, many of these being used by showmen when they were sold by the War Department after the hostilities. Scammell also produced a large number of heavy-duty trailer fire pumps.

In 1949/50 the ex-military Pioneer was redesigned for civilian use and named Mountaineer. Production of a well-designed range of rigid and tractor units was marketed during the next six years, but in 1955 Scammell was bought out by Leyland, which wisely kept the Watford plant in operation without radical or drastic changes.

The big 30ton bonneted Highwayman tractor introduced in the mid-1950s was updated in the late 1950s and re-rated as 24ton gcw. In 1960 the Handyman made its appearance, and this was modified in 1964 with an Italian-designed cab as fitted to others in the Scammell range at that time, such as the rigid eight-wheeled 24ton gvw Routeman which first appeared in 1960, the same year as the Trunker 6×4 tractor unit entered production, and this again was updated in 1964.

In 1970 the Crusader 4×2 tractor was introduced but does not appear to have been too successful.

Today Scammell is the specialised division of Leyland producing heavy tractors and from the 1970s former Thornycroft models, such as the airport fire-fighting vehicle, the Nubian, and the Amazon 6×6 tractor for gross weights of up to 300ton and now fitted with the Leyland cab similar to the Landtrain series, are produced. Other current models include the Constructor and S26, covering a range from 24tonnes gvw to 300tonnes gcw, both of which feature the Leyland C40 cab.

Below: A classic Scammell tractor and semi-trailer supplied in 1954. It was later called the Highwayman. It had a Gardner six-cylinder engine and was popular with many operators. The tanker could carry 4,000gal of petroleum spirit and was under 22ton gross weight.

Above: Eight years on from the previous illustration this Highwayman has the more modern cab with wrap-round screen and increased visability at the lower corners. It was powered by the Leyland O.680 diesel developing 181bhp. The 3,800gal tank was built by Thompson Bros.

Below: This Constructor model is hauling a 180ton casting from Sheffield to Liverpool for machining.

Left: The Contractor range was introduced in 1964 especially to meet the demands of the heavy haulage specialist. There were seven basic models either 6×4 or 6×6 and with a choice of engines and gearboxes.

Below: A Routeman rigid-eight featuring the Michelotti-styled cab which was fitted to several models. This 30-tonner has an extended wheelbase, and handles loads of up to $17\frac{1}{2}$ ton. The Routeman can be fitted with several different engines and gearbox combinations.

Above: A 1968 Trunker II operating with a tandem axle tipping trailer for a 32ton gcw. This version was powered by a Leyland engine but there were many variants.

Left: A Crusader 6×4 tractor destined to be shown at the Commercial Motor Show in 1968. There was also a 4×4 version, and again there were many engine and gearbox options for the operator.

Above right: The familiar mechanical horse — the Scammell Scarab in its postwar form. These vehicles were always popular with the railway companies.

Right: The Townsman was the replacement for the Scarab. This new unit had a glass fibre cab and a number of outstanding design and mechanical features.

RAIL FREIGHT
5357G
M
14332 GT3C
M
RAIL FREIGHT
SUR 925
SCAMMELL

AAU 399B
3G
5588
S

Seddon 1938-1974

Entering the commercial vehicle manufacturing field in 1937, Foster and Seddon had previously been engaged in the distribution and repair of vehicles for some 18 years. Their first vehicle was a forward-control lightweight 6ton chassis fitted with a Perkins P6 diesel engine. It was just proving popular with operators when the war called a halt to further production. After the war the model reappeared and the firm became Seddon Lorries from 1947. The range was expanded and in 1950 a small 3ton lorry powered by a Perkins engine appeared and two years later a normal control 25cwt and 30cwt van (known as the 25 range) which incorporated many glass-fibre body panels was produced. This did not gain popularity, although the 3tonner remained in production until 1963.

Styling changes took place in 1956 when wrap-round windscreens were fitted and a year later some models could be obtained with plastic cab panels. The emphasis shifted to the heavier models and in 1956/7 a 14ton gvw chassis (the Mk 15) was put on the market. Heavier rigids entered production during 1965/6 with Motor Panels cabs while in 1967 a tractor unit for 28ton gross and 32ton appeared powered by Rolls-Royce or Gardner engines.

Seddon was able to take over the old-established firm of Atkinson in 1970 and within two years a new heavy range was designed. Vehicles were still using the Seddon name, but in 1974 the new concern was acquired by International Harvester and became Seddon Atkinson — see next chapter.

Below: A Seddon 6ton platform lorry powered by a Perkins P6 diesel engine and following the basic design of the first Seddon produced.

Above: A Mk 7 3ton tractor fitted with a Perkins P4 engine and coupled to a Carrimore low-loading semi-trailer used as a mobile showroom. The overall length of the unit was 33ft, it was 7ft 6in wide and the overall height was 10ft. It was supplied in 1954.

Below: A Mk 7L 3ton four wheel platform lorry.

Below: The forward control 25cwt van which was introduced in 1953 and fitted with a Perkins P3 engine.

Bottom: A model 30 tractor with Gardner 6LX engine developing 150bhp.

Above: A DD8 model 8×4 with power assisted steering for a $16\frac{1}{4}$ton payload. It was fitted with the Gardner 6LX engine.

Below: New in 1966 was the Seddon 16 tractor units. This version was powered by a Perkins V8 diesel engine producing 170bhp and with a wheelbase of 9ft 3in it operated at 25ton gvw.

Above: The 13/4 model of 1965/6 had a 14ft 8in wheelbase, and was fitted with a body 21ft long by 8ft 6in high. It was designed for a payload in excess of 8ton.

Below: The Seddon Mk 15 for 11ton gross weight. It was powered by a Gardner 4LK engine and was one of the last types of Seddon cab to be produced before the company amalgamated with Atkinson.

Seddon Atkinson 1974-To date

The American concern International Harvester already had a European interest in commercial vehicles as it acquired a stake in the Dutch concern DAF. It also made a small effort in the UK in 1965-9.

When it acquired Seddon Atkinson in 1974 the range was already well established and continued unaltered in spite of rumours that all models would have the same cab design as DAF. In 1975 new heavyweight four, six- and eight-wheeled rigids in the 400 range were in production as well as a 4×2 articulated tractor unit for 32ton gcw. A year later a lighter four-wheel rigid for 17ton playload was offered being designated the 200 series and powered by the International D358 engine. The 300 series appeared in 1978 which was a six-wheeled rigid for 24ton gvw. In 1982 the 200, 300 and 400 series were superseded by the similar but improved 201, 301 and 401 respectively.

At the time of writing International Harvester was experiencing financial difficulties and there was much speculation about a takeover of Seddon Atkinson by another group, several of which were interested.

Below: A Seddon Atkinson 200 series tipper for 16ton gvw with a 12ft 6in wheelbase. All the 200 series are equipped with an International D358 diesel engine developing 134bhp.

Above: A series 200 16ton gvw van which has a 24ft long alloy body. It is one of seven supplied in May 1977.

Right: The series 400 shown here has a 24ft long body and a 17ft 6in wheelbase to carry heavy test weights for the weighbridge industry. It is powered by a Gardner 6LXB engine, one of several options for the 400 series.

Below right: A turbocharged Gardner engine developing 270bhp is fitted to this 1981 Series 400. All the 400 series have tilt cabs.

Sentinel 1906-1957

The Scottish engineering firm of Alley and McLellan established the Sentinel steam lorry in 1906 moving from Polmadie, Glasgow to Shrewsbury in 1918. The Sentinel quickly gained popularity and by the mid-1920s the company was producing a six-wheeler for a 15ton payload, while in the 1930s the vehicles had modern equipment such as electric speedometers, electric lights, power take-off and self-stoking boilers. Their speed and absence of noise was quite remarkable.

During the war the firm was prominent in experiments and the manufacture of gas-producer trailers to help overcome the diesel and petrol shortage.

The last steam wagons were produced in 1949 as an export order for the Argentine, the UK market having fallen since the late-1930s.

In the period covered by this book the firm concentrated on diesel lorries and from 1946 manufactured a four-wheel forward-control 7/8ton vehicle with underfloor engine. A few six-wheel chassis were also produced for a 10ton load. All the vehicles had the Sentinel-Ricardo horizontal diesel engine mounted on a frame behind the modern-looking cab.

In 1957 the firm was acquired by Transport Vehicles (Warrington) Ltd which took over the stocks of existing chassis, some of which were fitted with the Commer two-stroke engine in the conventional location. Production finally ceased when all existing stocks of chassis had been used.

Below: A Sentinel model 4/4DV 7-8tonner showing the position of the underfloor engine. This was the standard Sentinel design.

Above: Two 7-8ton models having a 16ft wheelbase and a 22ft long platform. These show the redesigned cab which appeared on later models.

Below: The 6/6DV six-wheeler for 12ton payloads. It is fitted with a four-cylinder engine and has a 21ft 10in platform length.

Shelvoke and Drewry 1923-To date

The firm was started in 1923 by Harry Shelvoke and J. S. Drewry, both ex-employees of Lacre, and its first production was a small forward-control vehicle with a 2ton payload and 20in-diameter wheels called the Freighter. The driver half stood literally in-between the transverse engine and on his right and left had handles similar to a tram controller, one of which steered the vehicle and the other effected the speed change and reverse. The gearbox was a semi-automatic unit, with three speeds in either direction! The vehicles were popular as they had a low floor height of only 1ft 11in and this made them eminently suitable for refuse collecting and local delivery work. From 1932 until 1939 the firm also produced the Latil Tractor under licence from the French firm.

In 1946 the W-type Freighter appeared and this had conventional controls. It was again popular with municipal authorities and many of the chassis were fitted with a rear-loading tipping body which compressed the refuse by gravity in its barrel-shaped shell. From 1961 the Pakamatic rear loading body in which the refuse was compressed by a mechanical ram was built. The latest type (from 1970) is the Revopak in which the contents are compressed by a rotary action. In both cases unloading was accomplished by a normal tipping action and gravity. The vehicles are powered by a variety of engines including Ford, Leyland and Perkins.

In 1971 S&D became part of the Butterfield-Harvey Group and from 1973 has used Motor Panels cabs on some of its products. From 1975 it instigated the Special Purpose Vehicles division which produces 4×4 and 6×4 off-the-road vehicles such as drilling rigs, military vehicles, airport crash tenders and from 1976 fire appliances. Some of the latter are built in conjunction with Carmichael of Worcester, which has undertaken the bodywork. Engines which can be fitted include the Cummins V8, the Perkins V8 or the Rolls-Royce straight-eight.

Below: This W-type refuse collector was produced in 1947 and is typical of the Shelvoke and Drewry design of that time. It had a four-cylinder side-valve engine of 67bhp. The cab could seat six loaders plus the driver. The side loading body had an 18cu yd capacity.

Thornycroft

The origins of Thornycroft go back to 1864 when John Isaac Thornycroft began building steam-driven launches for river work. Later he turned his attentions to steam-driven road vehicles and in 1896 produced a steam van, but he kept his marine interests. Early experiments with petrol and paraffin engines kept Thornycroft to the forefront of engineering and its J-type lorries of World War 1 fame were continued for civilian use for many years. In the 1930s Thornycroft made vehicles from 2ton to 15ton and for a wide variety of uses, which were extremely popular with operators both large and small. It also produced some vehicles for specialised work.

The War Department ordered some 5,000 vehicles during the last war, including the 4×4 Nubian and later the 6×4 Amazon model.

In 1948 the range was the Nippy 3ton, Sturdy 5/6ton, Sturdy 8ton tractor, the Amazon 12ton six-wheeler and the Trusty 15ton eight-wheeler. In 1950 the 12ton Trident rigid vehicle was introduced and the Sturdy revamped and called the Sturdy Star; the word 'Star' was also applied to the Nippy model. Shortly after this a new pressed-steel cab was introduced to the smaller vehicles in the range and this cab was shared with Guy Motors, although the two firms were not connected in any way.

The Nippy Star was replaced by the Swift and the Sturdy Star by the Swiftsure in 1957 when the Mastiff four-wheeled rigid seven-tonner appeared. In 1959/60 a new attractive cab with pronounced rounded corner panels was put on the market, but before they had become too familiar, Transport Equipment (Thornycroft) Ltd — to give the company its full title — was taken over by AEC and the range was trimmed down to the Nubian model and some special purpose vehicles. Eight years later the Basingstoke works were sold and all production transferred to Scammell at Watford.

Mention must be made of the Mighty Antar and Big Ben tractor units which were produced for special purposes and the haulage of indivisible loads. The former was designed for oil-field work but was also used by heavy haulage operators for gross weights in excess of 100ton. The latter vehicle appeared in 1954 as a six-wheel tractor for large loads of up to a maximum gross weight of 40ton using a new 11.33litre oil engine developing 155bhp from its six cylinders.

Below: A 1950 3ton Nippy lorry, one of many supplied to British Railways. The former Great Western Railway operated a great number of Nippy 3ton vans.

Top: A 1954 Trusty 8×4 platform lorry for 15ton payload. The girder is 48ft long and weighs 13ton.

Above: The Trusty could also be purchased as a 4×2 tractor as shown here with a 3,200gal four compartment tanker trailer in 1955.

Above: A Trident 9cu yd tipper on an 11ft 6in chassis. Body dimensions were 11ft 6in long by 7ft wide by 3ft high. Note the almost identical cab to those fitted to certain Guy vehicles.

Below: The Swiftsure 1959 model which had an improved cab and external appearance. It had a 6-7ton payload capacity.

Top: Designed originally for export to oil field operators etc, this Mighty Antar is proceeding through Edmonton (North London) in 1950. A smaller version of the Antar was introduced in the late 1950s named the Big Ben which had similar external appearance.

Above: One of the last heavy goods designs to come out of the Basingstoke works before the company was acquired by AEC. This is a 1958 version of the Trusty eight-wheeler.

Trojan 1924-1962

Originally designed by L. H. Hounsfield and built by Leyland at its Kingston Works from 1924, the Trojan had chassisless construction, chain drive, solid tyres and a 10hp two-stroke engine. The first model had a carrying capacity of only 5cwt, but this was later uprated to 7cwt. Trojan manufactured vehicles itself at its Purley works from 1928 and a 10cwt version, basically similar to the 7cwt model appeared in 1930 which remained in production until 1942. In 1937 a more advanced design was produced. The vehicles were popular with local tradesmen, but were extensively used by the Brooke Bond Tea Company.

In 1947 a completely new 15cwt van was put on the market, still with a two-stroke engine but an alternative Perkins P3V was also offered. This model continued in production until the company ceased to manufacture in 1959. The last design appeared in 1958 and was a forward-control 25cwt model again using the Perkins diesel engine. It was not an outstanding success in the popularity poll, although some were fitted with minibus bodies.

Below: A Trojan series 7 one-ton van of 1957. It has a neat appearance with a wheelbase of 7ft 10in and an overall length of 13ft 11in. The Perkins P3V diesel engine developed 34bhp from its three cylinders and the vehicle was claimed to return 40mpg.

Vulcan

Reference to the dates in the heading of this chapter just make this entry eligible. Vulcan was formed in 1903 to produce commercial vehicles and buses, which it did with varying success, but never reached the top of the league. The firm merged with Tilling Stevens in 1931 and production was transferred to Maidstone where it continued, although few buses were ever manufactured and only a handful of coaches which were on a modified goods chassis. In 1953 Tilling Stevens was taken over by the Rootes Group, which already had Commer and Karrier vehicles, and it was decided that Vulcan would be absorbed into those companies. Thus the name disappeared. The range at that time consisted of a forward control 6ton vehicle usually fitted with a Perkins P6 diesel engine.

Right: Intended for unveiling at the 1939 Commercial Motor Show, this 6ton Vulcan platform lorry was available in 1941 under Ministry of Transport licence. Powered by a four-cylinder engine of 78bhp it was the standard production model until Vulcan manufacture ceased; there was however a more modern cab on some later models.

Above: The six-tonner had a 13ft wheelbase and 16ft body length. The dray illustrated is for the transport of crates of beers and mineral waters.

SHEEPY FLOUR MILLS
SHEEPY.
TELEPHONE
ATHERSTONE 2146.
VULCAN
CAY 911

Fire Appliances

Up to the mid-1930s the old type fire appliance with the crew standing in the open holding on to the side of the escape, or sitting on bench type seats reminiscent of the old horse bus 'knifeboard' seating, was commonplace. Then to give the firemen some protection from the elements and some degree of comfort, the enclosed or limousine type bodywork was adopted.

During the war Auxiliary Fire Service (AFS) used many hundreds of Austin K2 chassis with an open-backed van body, extending ladders on the roof and towing a trailer pump. Such units did valiant work during the blitz in all parts of the country. After the war the Home Office specified some Bedford S-type chassis for emergency work and these became known as the Green Goddess type. They carried a pump capable of delivering 1,000gal of water per minute and a 35ft extending ladder on the roof. They were called out during the firemen's strike in 1979/80.

Up to the 1950s the main manufacturer of chassis for fire appliances were Dennis and Leyland, later joined by AEC. In the 1970s the main makers were again Dennis partnered by ERF plus Ford and Dodge, but in the 1980s fashion swung again to Dennis, Ford and Shelvoke.

Visible warning was given by up to four blue flashing lights adopted from 1961 and the bell has

been superseded by the two-tone horn as an audible warning. Colour schemes have also changed, for the traditional red has given way to experiments in yellow, red and white, and it seems the latest is 'dayglo' red with polished aluminium panels and fittings for the lockers on the vehicle sides.

The modern appliance — which has to conform to Home Office specifications — carries much more equipment than its predecessors of a couple of decades ago. With the advent of greater use of road transport which now carries chemicals, dangerous and inflammable liquids in bulk, and generally a greater risk of a major calamity, the Fire Brigade has to be ready to tackle many incidents which may not be actual fires. Again the modern forms of furniture and decorations can mean that if there is a fire poisonous smoke and fumes may have to be combatted, therefore breathing apparatus for all the crew has to be carried, along with foam making equipment and a host of other specialised gear to cope with the differing contingencies.

The term fire appliance — it should never be called an 'engine' — is used in the general sense and envelops many differing types of specialised vehicles — pump/escapes, turntable ladders, emergency tenders, hose-laying lorries, mobile control rooms and salvage corp tenders.

In addition to the normal appliances on the roads there are specialised vehicles which have been developed for airport and airfield services, but being off-the-road vehicles are beyond the scope of this book.

Left: A typical example of a postwar fire appliance of 1949. This Dennis dual purpose vehicle was built to the specification of the Central Fire Brigades Advisory Committee and the Home Office. It was powered by a Rolls-Royce eight-cylinder 150bhp petrol engine giving the appliance a maximum speed of 60mph and acceleration from 0 to 40 in 30sec. The laden weight was 8ton and overall length 27ft 6in with a wheelbase of 13ft 6in. It carried a 100gal water tank for the $\frac{3}{4}$in rubber first aid hose which pumped at 25gal/min.

Top: A Bedford general purpose appliance supplied to the Fife Fire Brigade in 1958. The whole of the front, cab roof, engine cowling and panel is polyester resin. The body was built by HCB (Hampshire Car Bodies).

Centre: ERF constructed the bodywork on this Dodge K850 chassis for the West Riding Fire Brigade appliance based at Wakefield.

Bottom: An ERF chassis fitted with Metz turntable ladder for Hampshire Fire Brigade.

Above left: An AEC Marquis fire appliance which is typical of a style built in the late 1950s. This was supplied to Leicester, but many were supplied to other Brigades including London. It is similar to the Dinky Toy model.

Left: A Ford D1317 chassis with Cheshire Fire Engineering body for this water tender/ladder appliance supplied to Shropshire Fire Service in 1980. The chassis is not standard, but developed for the purpose by Ford's special vehicle engineering department and meets Home Office specification. It is powered by a Perkins 8.8litre V8 diesel producing 168bhp. The appliance carries 400gal of water, a 35ft two-section ladder and crew of six. Its gross laden weight is 11ton.

Above: The Dennis R series of which there are many variants. This is a 1977 product.

Centre right: Introduced in 1978 and now in use by many authorities including Surrey and Middlesex is this Shelvoke 4×2 chassis fitted with the four-door crew cab especially designed for fire use. The rest of the body and equipment was supplied by Cheshire Fire Engineering Ltd.

Bottom right: The Land Rover was one of the smallest fire appliances. The 2litre engine drives the 150/ 200gal/min pump, and also supplied the first-aid reel from the 40gal tank mounted amidship. The all-up weight was 2ton.

Municipal Vehicles

Having devoted a short chapter to fire appliances, it is only right that a selection of ambulances and refuse collecting vehicles also be shown. While not so glamorous they also play their part for the community.

Changes have obviously been made in the period covered by this book, and as far as ambulances are concerned they have become more specialised, with plastics playing an important part in the interior fittings. Refuse collecting vehicles have become more hygenic and the days of the side-loaders with all the dust and dirt flying on the breeze have virtually disappeared.

Below: A Lever-bodied Bedford in 1952 and now looking quite dated.

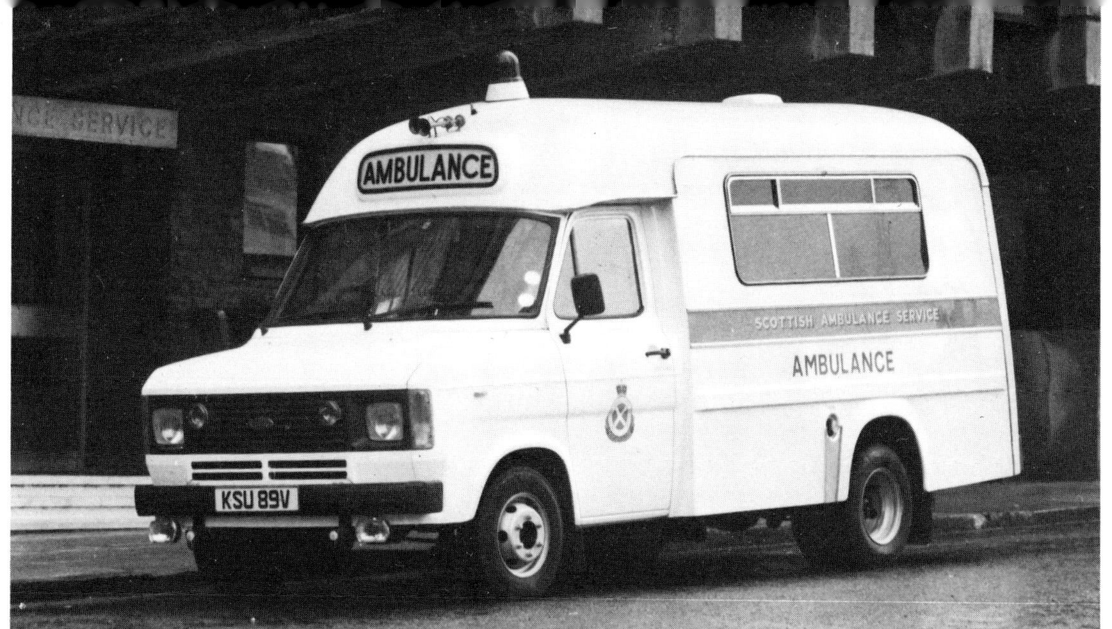

Top: A 1980 Ford Transit with Wadham Stringer body. A Ford SVO 3litre V6 petrol engine is fitted.

Above: The Karrier $1\frac{1}{2}$ton chassis (now Dodge) from the Walk-through van is fitted with a Dennis Ambulance body and is popular with many authorities having a top speed of about 60mph from the six-cylinder petrol engine of 2.96litre capacity which develops 85bhp.

Top: The Morris FG series with wheelbase of 10ft 9in has a body by Wadham Stringer. This model dates from 1963.

Above: A Range Rover with ambulance body is used by several hospitals and private institutions.

Above: A typical example of a small side-loading refuse collector of 1952. This Karrier Bantam had a capacity of 7cu yd.

Below: In marked contrast to the above is this 1976 Karrier 8ton 13ft 6in wheelbase chassis with Glover, Webb & Liversidge continuous loading refuse collection body.

Above: A Leyland Boxer chassis with Perkins engine and Jack Allen Colectomatic refuse collection body as supplied to the London Borough of Lambeth in 1981.

Right: A Ford D500 with Eagle 800gal gulley and cesspool emptier.

Breakdown Vehicles

The style and operation of breakdown vehicles has changed considerably over the years. The modern commercial and passenger vehicle has become more reliable, but mechanical troubles can never be ruled out and unfortunately there is always the problem of accidents. which with the coming of the motorways can be more serious when they happen. As legislation has permitted larger and heavier commercial vehicles on the roads, so the breakdown unit has had to follow suit. Nowadays it is a specialised vehicle, with — it is hoped — a specialised crew. The days of the simple rear mounted crane, often on an old lorry chassis, have gone except in a few cases for the towing of private cars or light vans.

For a couple of decades after the last war, many operators of breakdown cranes used vehicles purchased from ex-WD sales, and a selection of ex-service vehicles could be seen operating in a civilian organisation but they have now almost disappeared from the scene. Many operators of such vehicles were ex-servicemen who were starting out in business, some with improvised home-made equipment. It was also the time of the birth of the 'accident pirates', and these small firms and individuals would position their vehicle in a strategic position alongside a main arterial road, listening to police traffic messages on short-wave radio. They often arrived at the scene of an accident before the emergency services! The 'pirates' usually had small vehicles, little equipment, and often even less knowledge of lifting and recovering a vehicle from a difficult position.

It was not so long ago that the only really heavy recovery vehicle belonged to the County Fire Brigade or some of the larger municipal transport undertakings, or one of the specialist transport contractors such as Pickfords, although the latter usually only dealt with its own vehicles, unless in an emergency if received a police request for assistance.

The modern heavy recovery vehicle is usually fitted with four-wheel drive, large power-operated winches, twin-boom cranes (developed from an Amercian idea), heavy-duty hydraulic jacks, oxy-acetylene cutting apparatus and a host of other equipment. A recent innovation is a large inflatable air-cushion to absorb the impact and minimise further damage when righting an overturned vehicle.

Below: An ex-American Diamond Tank Transporter unit working as a civilian recovery vehicle. The Hercules diesel engine still powered the unit which could tow up to 50ton. Maximum lift was 12ton and maximum on winch pull 17ton, increased by 10 or even 20 times by the use of pulley blocks.

Above: The modern recovery vehicle is exemplified by this 1978 Ford 4×2 Transcontinental fitted with powerful equipment and lifting and winching facilities.

Below: For smaller jobs and private cars the Ford Transit is ideal and this version is fitted with a Holmes Cadet 1000 crane. The Cadet is available with electrical winching or with a lift chain and boom end, and features an electro-hydraulic boom lift for easy manoeuvrability.

Battery Electrics

By reason of carrying its own power supply in the form of a large bank of batteries, such vehicles have remained in the light van class. In demand prewar and, of course, during the war when petrol was rationed, their popularity declined except for milk rounds. Their limited range and low speeds have restricted them to local delivery work.

However with recent developments in battery technology and electric motors which use less current, and spurred on by the anti-pollution campaigners there has been an increase in experimental activity. Ford Transits have been converted and have been tried by the Post Office, while the North Western Electricity Board even has a battery driven Leyland Boxer van. An experimental taxi and even a full-size single-deck bus towing a trailer containing the batteries have been in use. Now the Bedford CF, Leyland Sherpa and Dodge 50-series vans are all available in battery-electric form, but a high purchase price, limited range and reduced payload have conspired against large-scale production.

It is possible that in another two decades, the battery electric vehicle may prove more feasible and commonplace.

Below: A Smiths NCB one-ton van for British Rail. It has a range of 37 miles and a maximum speed of 18mph fully laden on a level road.

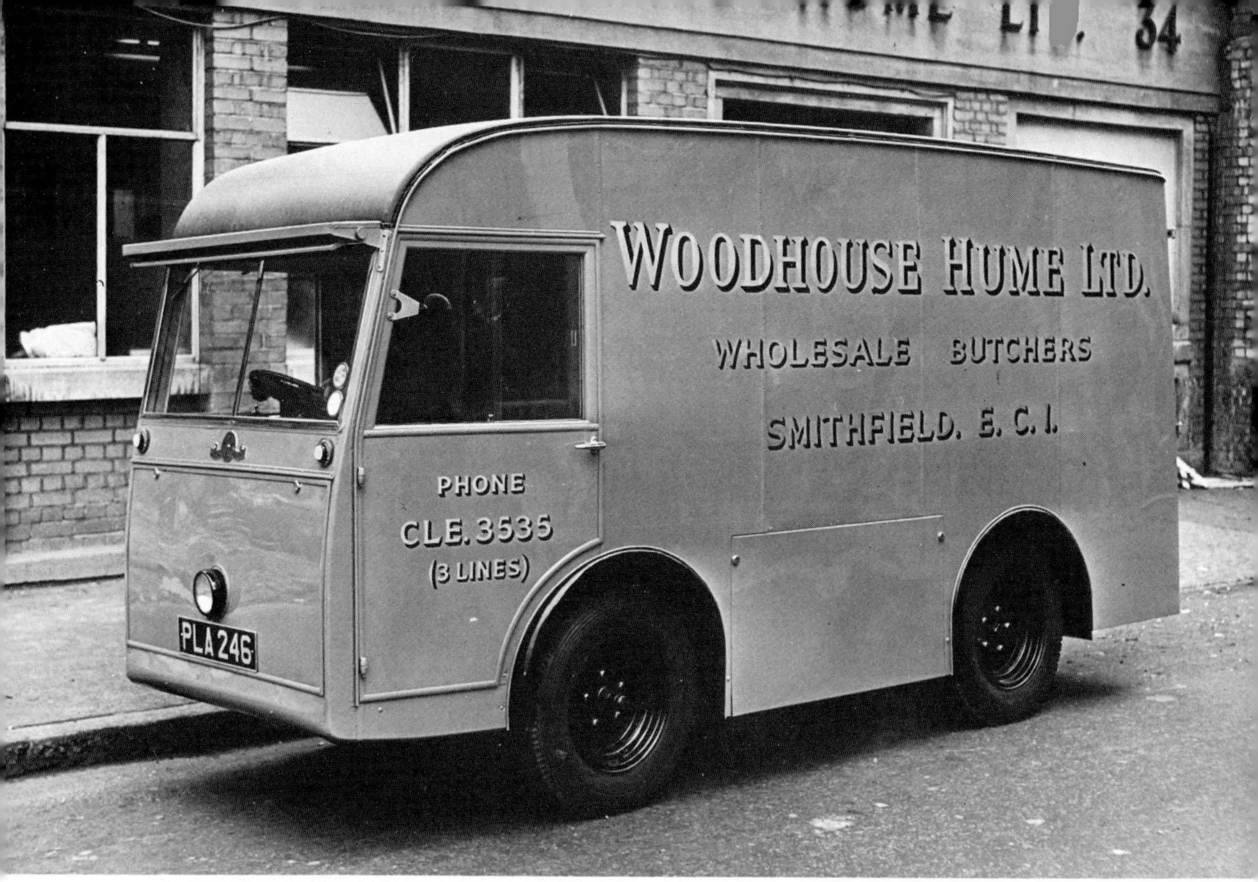

Above: A one-ton Morrison Electricar of 1954.

Left: The ubiquitous milk float. This one is a Wales & Edwards 25cwt long wheelbase chassis supplied in 1958 with a speed of 12-14mph

Above right: A modern battery electric vehicle in use by the Post Office, supplied by Crompton Electric Vehicles.

Right: The latest concept in battery electric vehicles. A Bedford CF van/minibus in experimental use for local service. Several experimental vehicles are being so designed with good performance being acclaimed.

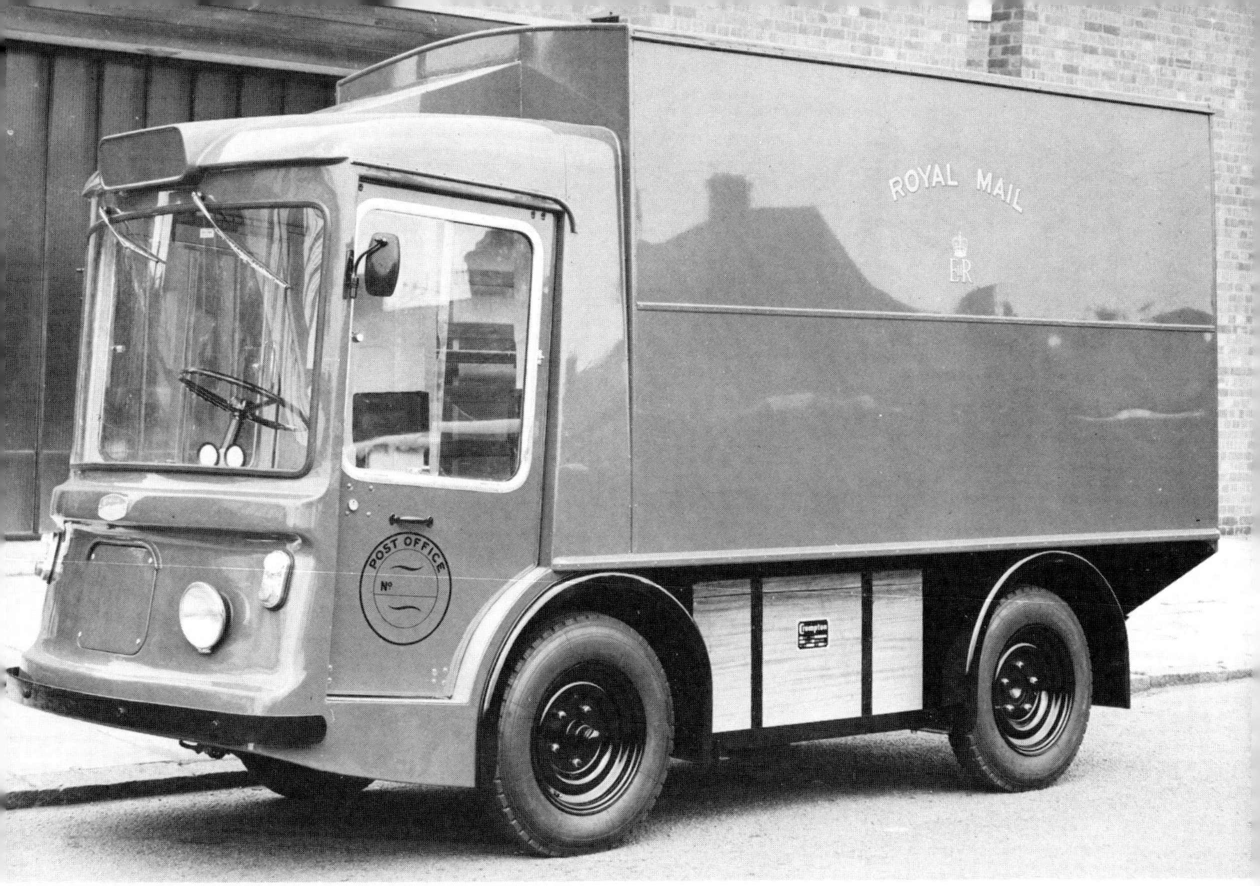
ROYAL MAIL
POST OFFICE
No

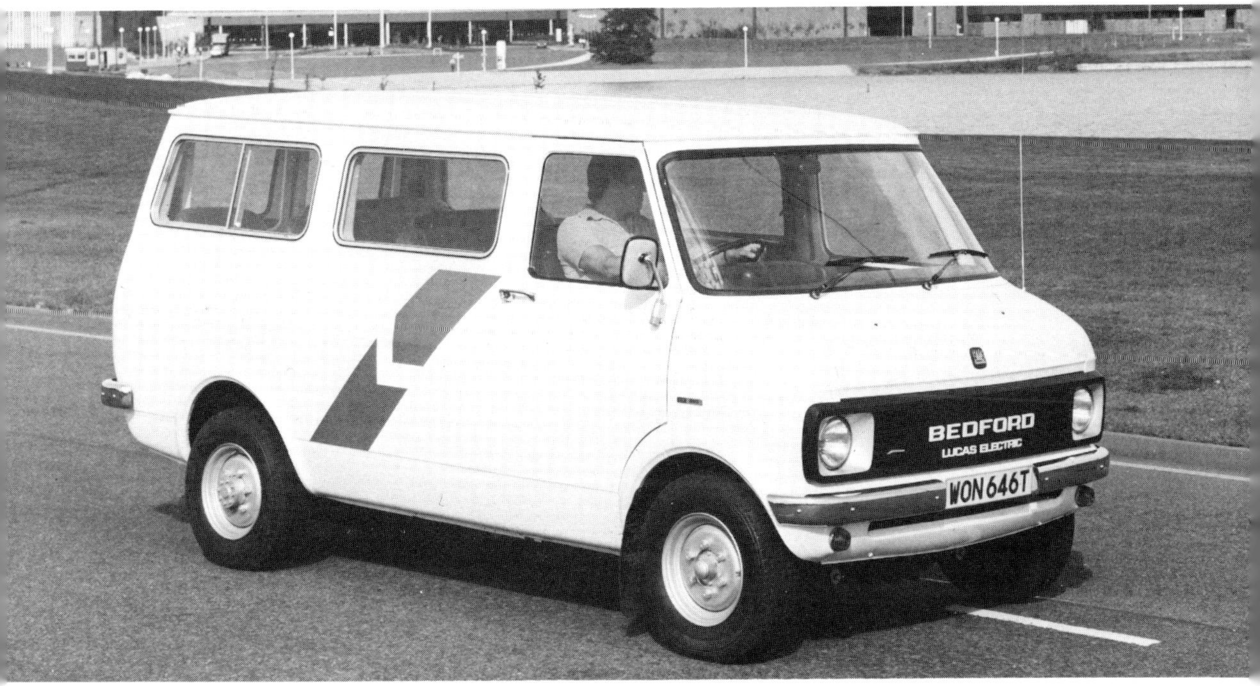
BEDFORD
LUCAS ELECTRIC
WON 646T

Fairground Vehicles

Road transport is the life-blood of the travelling showman, whose transport is usually varied and interesting. As the actual mileage covered in a year is small by comparison with a haulage business, showmen inevitably purchase their transport vehicles secondhand from recognised haulage contractors or operators and this is where many fine vehicles end their days, long after their compatriots have left the general road haulage field.

Many of the vehicles are rebodied to suit the specialised loads they will be conveying; often the body is taken from a previous vehicle, and there are still a few examples of wooden-planked van-type bodies in existence — the body sometimes being three times the age of the chassis it is upon. The modifications made are often ingenious and demontrate the competence of the showman as a mechanical engineer.

By the very nature of the loads carried the most popular vehicle is the diesel powered prime mover or tractive unit which can carry a generating set where the articulated coupling gear was placed and can also haul up to three large trailers, each carrying a maximum load.

A large 'ride' such as a Dodgem set usually requires at least two rigid eight-wheelers each pulling a massive trailer, plus the prime mover (with generating equipment) pulling two trailers — often the pay box and control desk plus the operator's own living wagon (or caravan).

Until recently articulated semi-trailer units were not favoured by showmen because of the difficulty of manoeuvring especially over rough terrain and their inability to pull another trailer. However, over the past 10 years or so, new rides and machines have been designed and built for their base or platform to be permanently fixed to a semi-trailer. Such rides as lifting paratroopers, satellites and their associated meteorites, hurricane jets etc are arranged to fold up to the sides of the main unit on the semi-trailer to make a compact although unwieldly looking load which is then coupled direct to the tractive unit via the normal fifth wheel.

Current vehicle legislation has made it prudent (and sometimes necessary!) for the showmen to have more up-to-date vehicles then hitherto, thus many of the real antiques such as the Tilling Stevens, ex-WD vehicles etc have virtually disappeared, but the fairground can still have some interesting and unique examples of specialised transport.

Below: This 1944 Leyland van was originally owned by Callard & Bowser and now with a Showman. Seen at Wanstead Flats in 1981.

Above right: The ex-Army AEC Matador 4×4 gun tractor is becoming quite rare on the fairground nowadays. This one was owned by Biddalls and is seen in 1965.

Right: A little bit of glamour on the scene! Exquisite signwriting on Bob Wilson's Atkinson van at Ealing in 1967.

Below: A home-built body on this eight-wheeler with distinctive lettering. Note the colossal overhang at the rear of the van.

BENSON'S
BENSON'S
MODERN AMUSEMENTS
PHONE
4366
DORKING
SCAMMELL
SHOWTRAC
FDL 111

FORREST'S
AMUSEMENTS
FORREST'S
MODERN AMUSEMENTS
ONTOUR
NUC953

Above left: A Scammell design of 1946 especially for the Showman – The Showtrac. The engine is a Gardner 6LW developing 102bhp. The gross train weight is 45ton and the diesel engine inside the body at the rear drives a generator with a maximum output of 450A. There is also a winch and a ballast block for adhesion.

Left: A veteran AEC Mammoth Major eight-wheeled van in use by Forrests Amusements photographed on Blackheath in April 1973.

Above: A sign of the times! A Foden articulated unit with Henry Smith's complete and self- contained Flying Orbiter load. The semi-trailer forms the base of the machine when in use. Note the paybox in the centre. Seen at Newhaven in August 1978.

Centre right: Two dignified stalwarts of the fairground! Edwards's of Swindon with two Scammell tractors *The Lady Margaret* and *The Churchill.* Edwards names nearly all of its vehicles which are always immaculately turned out, lined and lettered. Note the levelling block of wood under one of the front wheels. Seen at Hampstead Heath in 1974.

Bottom right: A veteran Atkinson eight-wheeled van in use by John Biddall of London at Hampstead Heath.

Above: Living accommodation for fairground workers is provided by this ERF van with dormitory accommodation at the rear. It belongs to London Showman Fred Gray and seen in 1968 on Wimbledon Common.

Below: Another Scammell tractor of the type favoured by the petrol companies and now in fairground use. This nicely lettered version is owned by Armstrong's and about to reverse with a box trailer to pull it into position. Wanstead Flats in 1979.

Shell-Mex and B.P. Ltd
Shell Mex House, Strand, London
344 BGO